alain colas

around
the
world
alone

alain colas

around the world alone

Translated by
J. F. Bernard

BARRON'S/WOODBURY, NEW YORK

All inquiries should be addressed to:
Barron's Educational Series, Inc.
113 Crossways Park Drive
Woodbury, New York 11797

Library of Congress Catalog Card No. 78-18195

International Standard Book No. 0-8120-5219-6

Library of Congress Cataloging in Publication Data

Colas, Alain, 1943-
  Around the world alone.

  Translation of Cap Horn pour un homme seul.
  1. Manureva (Trimaran)   2. Colas, Alain, 1943-
3. Voyages around the world.   I. Title.
G440.M316C6413   910'.41'0924 [B]   78-18195
ISBN 0-8120-5219-6

PRINTED IN THE UNITED STATES OF AMERICA

*This book is dedicated to
my comrades: the men of the
tall ships of yesteryear,
those unpolished noblemen
with gnarled hands; and the
men who race on the open seas
today, who are the heirs
of those seamen long dead.*

Contents

1

"When I'm grown up . . ."

When I was a child, I had a recurring dream. I was sitting on a chair with my feet on the ground.

On one of my birthdays—I think it was my seventh—my father built me a diminutive armchair. As it happened, it was low enough for my feet to rest on the ground when I was sitting on it. My father, in giving me what I wanted, had taught me the meaning of hope.

It was probably the first time I realized something very important: that dreams are meant to be fulfilled. That was the best gift that my father ever gave me.

"When I'm grown up." I used to repeat that phrase over and over again, like any child; and I think I learned from it to profit from the encounters I was to have in later life. There are moments in our lives when we become suddenly aware, as though our understanding were illuminated by a sudden flash of lightning, that we have just crossed a frontier. We know, at that moment, that we have climbed another rung on our chosen ladder. It may be nothing more than a child's armchair, or it may be something much more serious. In either case, we are aware that we have grown.

Anyone who gives himself wholeheartedly to sailing, to sailing on the open sea, to transoceanic sailing competition, knows there is one place that he will have to go if he has any sense at all of the tradition that he has inherited. To anyone who knows the sea, it is not necessary even to name that place. It is a Mecca, an almost mythic place that every seaman carries in his heart. But, you don't decide to try Cape Horn the way that you would decide to go for a swim.

All sailors want, some day, to have a try at the "long route" around the world. At the same time, we all know that the preparation for such an undertaking is long, slow, and arduous. It requires patience: the patience and endurance of the sea itself. Only then can we feel that we are "grown up" and worthy of the ordeal.

Or, to put it simply, we are willing to go through all the preparation simply because it is something we want to do. Because we feel that we must. Because there comes a time in a seaman's life when there is no other way of expressing himself.

To the sailor, Cape Horn is a bit of bravura, the most beautiful page in the history of the sea. It represents the saga of navigators who, for a moment, became Roland in the pass at Roncesvalles. To sail around Cape Horn is to pass the supreme test of seamanship. It is to become one of that heroic—and sometimes anonymous—group that is the subject of ancient legends.

Having said that, I must add that I had set goals for myself more precise than a vague intention of rounding Cape Horn. I wanted to do something that no one else had ever done. As far as sailing was concerned, this meant taking a trimaran around the world by way of the three capes—with or without a crew. I also wanted to follow in the wake, so to speak, of Sir Francis Chichester by equaling the time of the great clipper ships of the nineteenth century.

The record of the old British lion (160 days for the voyage

to Sydney and 120 to return) seemed to me to be within my capability. After all, I had a highly perfected weapon: my boat. And, more important perhaps, there existed between my boat and myself a perfect accord—the same kind of accord we sometimes see between a jockey and his horse; we say that the jockey and the horse are part of each other.

The time had come for me, without over-romanticizing the situation, to measure myself against the clipper ships and, in the measuring, perhaps to win my golden spur.

In 1873, the great English sailing ship *Cutty Sark* set out on her maiden voyage to Sydney. She reached it after sixty-nine days at sea. It was a record that left all rival clipper ships far behind; a record that the ship retained on each successive crossing.

A hundred years later, another sailing vessel left the Channel for the same destination. This one was carrying no merchandise. She had no crew, for she had none of the great square sails of the clippers for a crew to handle. There was only one man aboard an aluminum boat with a steel frame and synthetic, Tergal,* line; a man whose only cargo was the determination to follow in the wake of the clipper ships regardless of the cost—all to see if a man could still sail around the southern capes as fast as his ancestors did.

It has been a long time since the propeller replaced sails on the commercial ships on every sea of the globe. But between cruises and races the pleasure sailor still dreams of emulating the traditions to which he regards himself as heir. He still has visions of the fabled runs of tall ships with sails billowing like great clouds against the sky.

Cape Horn. The name itself seemed to stir the sail of the trimaran, becalmed in the night as it returned from Newport

---

*Brand name of a polyester fiber manufactured in France and used for lines and ropes. (*Tr.*)

3

bearing the laurels of winning the Singlehanded Transatlantic Race.

To win the Transatlantic Race is to breathe the air of Olympus, more rarified even than that at the top of Mt. Everest. It is to empty, in one great swallow, the cup of a joy so great that, even when the clouds begin to dissipate and the winner has to return to earth, he remains stunned by the very intensity of it.

Except—except that, behind the rose-colored haze rising from one's victory, one sees looming another mountain. And this one is higher, more beautiful, more majestic. It has the shape of a cone, and its slopes are wild and alien. Waves pound at its base with savage force; and there one finds written one of the harshest pages of the story of human adventure. It is called Cape Horn, and it stands like a dark sentinel, marked by grandeur and by tragedy, in the glacial solitude at the extreme tip of the South American continent, at the crossroads of the great lanes of the sailing ships.

Once the vision was glimpsed, it seemed that the way to attain it boiled down merely to a few details, like finding a boat. I tried. My efforts usually began, "Dear Sir," and always put the same question more or less straightforwardly: "Have you thought about rounding the Horn, and, if so, are you looking for a crewman?"

Invariably, the reply came: "Indeed not. Why on earth would anyone want to round the Horn? I mean, that's not the sort of thing one does today, old boy."

All right, I told myself, eyeing the sour grapes. Let them keep their boats. I'll work something out for myself, somehow. Something that won't have anything to do with them.

What I had in the back of my mind—since there seemed to be no other way, in any case—was a solitary voyage following the most direct course, with a stop (a port of call, some would insist) midway. That is how it was done in the old days, when sailing was a livelihood rather than a sport and the seas were populated by workers instead of yachtsmen; when ships rounded the Cape of Good Hope in search of wool, gold, and wheat from the lands of the fabled East and then returned by way of Cape Horn.

Let me go back for a moment—without repeating the story of *Pen Duick IV*—and give a brief account of my 1972 victory in the Transatlantic Race. I'd also like to tell you about my affair with that particular boat.

I remember very well the first time I set eyes on her. It was in 1968. In fact, it was during the month of May, when French students swarmed into the streets of Paris and manned the barricades. I had just returned from Australia to find Paris in turmoil and the students converted into experts on throwing paving stones. Since I had no taste for that particular sport, it seemed to me in much better taste—and certainly more useful—to go to Lorient, where my old boss, Eric Tabarly, was getting his boat ready for the Singlehanded Transatlantic in June.

At that time, Tabarly's spiderlike trimaran looked a bit like a seafaring monster. As yet, no one had seen what something like the 128-foot *Vendredi 13* could do in the water. And disproportion was still disproportion: this boat was seventy feet long, with a beam of slightly over thirty-five feet. That this tub, with only one man on board, would try to race across the North Atlantic, which is one of the most difficult courses anywhere . . . well, it was more than most of us could imagine.

All sailors remember what happened during this third Transatlantic Race. *Pen Duick IV*, by then, had created a sensation and was the favorite to win until she collided with a cargo ship in the English Channel the very first night of the race. Tabarly was obliged to limp into Plymouth harbor for repairs. Sixty-eight hours later, he set out again. But this time, his anemometer was not functioning properly and Eric had to give it up.

The trimaran was, in effect, a prototype; it was an experimental model, and Eric had not had enough time to get all the bugs out before the race.

Once everything had been attended to on the boat, Eric set out again. This time, he was not alone. Olivier de Kersauson and I were also aboard. Almost immediately, we set a new record: ten days and eleven hours from the southern tip of Tenerife, in the Canary Islands, to Martinique. Our average speed was eleven knots, a somewhat better time than the previous record of twelve days and thirteen hours set by *Atlantic* during the "Emperor's Race" of 1905, between New York and Lizard Head.

For me, it was a period of blissful discovery. The boat was fantastic. She had even greater potential than I had expected when I first saw her on the launching ramp at Lorient.

Several months later, there occurred the famous Los Angeles-Honolulu run. This was at a time when the Transpacific Race was limited exclusively to single-hulled craft. In spite of this, one hour after the other boats had sailed out of Los Angeles harbor, Tabarly decided to catch up with the others and participate in the race.

At the time, I had no idea that the whole purpose of the race, for Eric, was to engage in a bit of commerce or that the reason we had intruded into this restricted race was to help Eric sell his boat. It was only when we reached Honolulu and I saw Eric nail a large FOR SALE sign on the mast that I understood what was going on.

It was also at that moment that an idea sprang, full grown, into my mind. I re-experienced the intense emotion that I had felt at Plymouth as I watched the boats sail out under my very eyes in the Transatlantic. I felt certain I would be able to handle this strange-looking trimaran alone and efficiently.

6

Even though there had been three of us when we sailed across the Atlantic, the fact was that, during each of my watches I was alone to do everything that had to be done. Each watch had been a sample of solo sailing—eight hours a day of being alone on the boat. Moreover, I had had the advantage of being able to observe an expert: Eric was winner of the 1964 race and his handling of the boat was enough to polish any rough edges I might still have had. In such circumstances, a seaman quickly develops certain ambitions. Fifty years ago, a competent first mate no doubt watched his captain and learned as much as he could, with the idea eventually of striking out on his own.

That, of course, was the logical reason why, between the times that I was sailing with Eric, I signed up as a crewman in as many races as I could. In 1969, for example, I was aboard Gaston Defferre's *Palynodie* when we won France's Mediterranean championship. Later, for the Fastnet, I was aboard *Coriolan;* after the race, the boat's owner, Christian de Galéa, asked me to sail the boat back to France for him.

What I was doing was learning the seaman's trade, even though on the way I was not always able to avoid the stumbling blocks that human beings create for other human beings. I felt that I had to assert myself. Then I had to cut a path for myself through the jungle known as "the world of yachting."

The smaller the dog, the louder he barks. And I was fairly small. I was something of an outsider to yachting specialists. I was not even from one of France's traditional maritime provinces; nor had I yet been at Trinité-sur-Mer or La Rochelle, the holy places of French yachting. Today, I can understand how it must have rubbed yachtsmen the wrong way to see me shamelessly sign on as a crew member aboard a prestigious boat. It was like an elevator operator in the Empire State Building offering to guide mountain climbers up Mt. Everest because he has experience at high altitudes.

Eric's FOR SALE sign did him little good in Honolulu. There were no buyers. We took the boat to Tahiti, and then to New Caledonia. Still no buyers.

Between sailings, I had returned to France to try to find financial backing that would enable me to buy the boat. I spent my time warming the chairs in the waiting rooms of banks, trying to interest publishers in my project, telling my story to all and sundry in the innocent belief that it was appealing enough to get me what I wanted. Even now, I'm astonished at how naïve that story was: "Once upon a time there was a sailor who had crossed the Atlantic on a large ship. He was first mate to a great captain, and he can swear by all the gods of the sea that it is really an extraordinary boat. The captain has now put this boat up for sale. And the first mate needs your help to buy it. . . ."

They probably believed me, but they didn't offer to help—despite the eloquence of the cards I had describing me as Tabarly's first mate. I was learning that reputations were not transferable.

There was only one thing left for me to do. Eric had asked me to take the boat to California for the Transpacific Race, and I had already sent in a letter of resignation to my employer. Even in the supersonic age, the idea of sailing the Pacific is the stuff of which dreams are made. My father, however, had taught me not to believe that dreams were dreams. Since that time, I had always regarded my dreams as realities.

Between *Pen Duick IV* and myself I had immediately sensed the existence of a relationship that left absolutely nothing to be desired. It was a relationship that did not have to be—indeed, could not be—explained, either to myself or to anyone else. For the moment, the price tag on this relationship was 225,000 francs—about $45,000. There was nothing I could do but accept Tabarly's offer to take the boat to California. Obviously,

I could not be simultaneously in Australia and at sea; and I did not hesitate for a moment between the two. I would go ahead with *Pen Duick IV*. And so, with virtually no assets but my belief in the boat, I made the step. I used my Australian savings as a down payment; for the balance, I managed to secure a bank loan, committing myself irrevocably to a series of installment payments. From that time on, I learned what it was to sweat out each payment. I experienced, too, the periodic dread of having the boat, of which I was the precarious owner, attached for nonpayment. Somehow, by turning out stories, photographs, illustrated articles, etc., I was able to meet this monthly obligation with fair regularity.

Thereafter, matters progressed in such a way that, somehow, one beautiful day in June 1972, I found myself in the starting line-up at Plymouth, ready for a solo dash as a participant in the Transatlantic.

The idea of entering the Transatlantic had developed naturally and gradually. No one sits down one day and declares: "Well, I'm going to win the Transatlantic," the way that a child says, "I'm going to be a fireman." Instead, little by little, below the level of consciousness, things fall into place in your mind. When a student of the piano has practiced his scales long enough, he feels the urge to be alone on stage with his instrument. In my case, it was as though I had caught a pass and saw a clear field ahead of me—and saw, too, that I was in good enough shape to outdistance any potential tackler.

As Eric Tabarly's mate, I had felt that I was living my life fully and enjoying every minute of it. I did not yet understand that the sea, which I was learning in Eric's company, was already challenging me at the personal level. I saw no further than the simple pleasure of sailing with a thoroughly competent seaman. Gradually, however, the joy of sailing around the world aboard this old, patched hull disappeared and was replaced first by the desires and longings common to all racers,

9

and finally by an overriding determination to be first at the finish line. The desire to become a really expert sailor is not the unhealthy offshoot of a desire for domination. For someone who practices and takes pleasure in his art, virtuosity is the logical product of a determination to go one step further. It is, in effect, the joyful reward of a job well done.

At the time of the Transatlantic, I was not exactly an inexperienced outsider. Behind me, there was a solo cruise; an unusual one that was, in fact, my real preparation for the Transatlantic: the voyage in the trimaran from Tahiti to Trinité-sur-Mer that lasted from December 1971 to February 1972. In Tahiti, I met Teura, the friend and companion who is still with me today. We decided that she would accompany me back to France. It seemed a marvelous opportunity: two people alone on the endless sea. . . . Unfortunately, nature decided otherwise. On the first leg of the voyage, between Tahiti and Mauritius, Teura was so seasick that she had to fly the rest of the way. Meanwhile, I would undertake the social and economic endurance test of a nonstop, solo cruise from Mauritius to France.

It was my first solo voyage. I was ready, in fact, to do anything, both for the mere pleasure of it and for the preparation that it afforded for the future. I rounded the Cape of Good Hope and sailed northward in the Atlantic, reaching Trinité-sur-Mer on February 19, 1972, after sixty-six days at sea. It was a record at the time for a solo voyage: 150 nautical miles per day over a 10,000-mile course. This represented a clear improvement over the records established by Eric in the Transatlantic. The one true exploit of my life as a seaman, I think, is contained in that solitary trek through difficult weather in a boat already tired from an around-the-world voyage; a trek through days and sleepless nights of sailing until my hands were so swollen that I could hardly move them. By the end of the voyage, I had lost twenty pounds.

This is how I ended the chapter of my book that had to do with this cruise: "I feel as if I weigh a ton, and I can think of only one thing: sleep. My eyes are swollen from lack of it. In my mind, I'm already at the starting line for the Transatlantic." And it was true. The 3,000 miles of the Transatlantic had already been covered during my preparatory solo from Tahiti. No one knew that I was ready; and everyone's favorite was the huge schooner, *Vendredi 13,* belonging to the Lelouch clan and piloted by Jean-Yves Terlain.

The story of that race has been told many times, and I will not tell it again. I have a marvelous memory of a voyage of twenty days, thirteen hours, and fifteen minutes; of records broken and, in mid-race, my extraordinary and absolutely impossible overtaking of *Vendredi 13* which, for me, was like a victory. The second and final victory, of course, was on Friday, July 7: "I was sitting in the cockpit, absolutely unable to move. I could feel the tears running down my cheeks. I remembered the year of dreaming and preparing, the sacrifices of my family, the support of my friends, the joys, the disappointments. Then I cut the line. I had won. I was living the most beautiful moment of my life."

I was, in fact, so happy that I could not express my feelings in words. I had not only won, I had won a race of experts. I had proved that my love affair with the trimaran was an affair of the heart as well as of the mind and that the heart is never wrong. I was now in a position to repay all my debts; for after the race itself, there is always the race for money: the telling and retelling of the race, the sale of articles and photographs, the writing of the book on the Transatlantic and of the voyage around the world that had not only preceded the Transatlantic but had, in reality, determined the outcome of it. One year after Newport, I was at last an independent man, master of my own boat. The chair was solid, and my feet were resting firmly on the ground. I was conscious of having "grown," and a new challenge was clearly outlined in the halo of the sun setting behind the hills of Newport across my bow. For my boat and myself, the time had come to measure ourselves against Cape Horn.

2

Manureva

Having weighed the risks and made a decision, I now had to do everything I could to ensure my success. But it was not simply a question of doing what I had decided to do. If I were going to tackle the three capes alone, aboard a multihull, there was much work to be done. I would have to "Cape Hornize" *Pen Duick IV*. This was especially necessary because, after her around-the-world voyage and the Transatlantic, the boat was celebrating her fiftieth anniversary—in thousands of miles, that is.

So, after Newport, there was a lot of hard work ahead. I had to transform the Transatlantic racer into a craft capable of sailing safely through dangerous seas, of surviving the gigantic waves of the fortieth and fiftieth latitudes—in a word, I had to turn *Pen Duick IV* into a vessel worthy of the great capes.

First I had to increase the boat's security by incorporating a number of modifications because there were specific problems to face in the upper latitudes. Books, narratives, and experience all were agreed in emphasizing the height of the waves at Cape Horn—waves that roll unbroken except by the Cape itself and the threshold of the Drake Strait separating Tierra del Fuego from the Antarctic continent. The danger seemed to be that the giant waves in the roaring forties—and their cousins in the fifties—would catch the bow in such a way as to raise the stern and capsize the boat, stern over bow. Moreover, since I had decided to complicate things by competing with the great clippers of the past (at a distance of one century), I had to increase *Pen Duick IV*'s potential for speed.

Once those things were taken care of, I hoped to be able to do something to "humanize" the living quarters of the boat. After all, I was going to spend several months there.

Having established the broad outlines of what I was going to do, and having covered a respectable number of pages with lists of things to do, to buy, or to search for, I put on my best necktie and headed for Paris.

After a long winter and a late spring, things began to look hopeful. I was finally able to put together what I needed from a technical as well as from a financial standpoint.

The victory at Newport, welcome as it was, had done little to assure my financial future. It had been enough, with a bit of stretching here and there, to wipe out past debts; or, as accountants say, to liquidate my liabilities.

There is much to remember from that period of intense preparation—a wealth of labor and generosity from which I was to benefit: the work done over and over again until the result was perfection, with no thought to the amount of time involved. Such care and diligence could not be repaid by mere money. I shall keep with me forever the memory of the young woman who sewed my storm sail: the sail that we use only when no other sail will hold in the wind while we must still fight against the storm. The image in my mind is of this girl, at the Tonnerre sailmakers in Lorient, her face serious, her body bent over the work upon which, after all, my fate might depend. She was the daughter, granddaughter, and great-granddaughter of fishermen. Into my sail she was sewing her heritage; her wages had little to do with it. Whether she sewed well or poorly, her pay at the end of the month would be the same. But she was sewing into my sail her very being, stitch by stitch. It was her respect for the sea, or perhaps the ancient longing, each restless day, of wives, mothers, and daughters to see the sailor come home from the sea, that she sewed into my sail.

A thousand times, on a thousand different occasions, I bore witness to the good will, care, and skill of everyone involved in my preparations. There was a welder who used his torch with a diligence that went beyond mere skill. He worked, so to speak, with his conscience, with the constant thought in his mind that a less-than-perfect seam might be the cause of a leak, and perhaps of a tragedy. There were all the technicians who gave me the benefit of their expertise; the businessmen and industrialists who gave me the use of their equipment; the organizations and manufacturers who gave me their patronage and enthusiasm, as if their sole aim were to help a young man who, in the final analysis (despite his carefully worded proposals) really had nothing to offer beyond an act of faith.

It might be useful here to say a word or two about the concept of "commercial sponsorship." Obviously, that term does not refer to traditional advertising campaigns in which a manufacturer buys space in newspapers, or "time" on radio or television, and launches a campaign whose impact in the marketplace can be determined with a degree of precision. Selling a product by such campaigns is the classic expression of the advertising concept. It progresses by predictable stages and, with luck, it accomplishes its specific aim. In other words, the traditional advertising campaign represents an investment on which the sponsor is assured, within reason, of a return.

It was not at all the same thing with the proposals of Alain Colas. It was a different kind of game, one in which the risks involved seemed greater than the possible return on any sponsor's investment. For example, I had financial agreements with R.T.L. (Radio-Television Luxembourg) and with Ricard (a French liquor producer) for broadcasting rights. They knew, and I knew, that there would certainly be times during the voyage when radio contact would be impractical or impossible. It was obvious to me that, in such cases, the motivation of my "sponsors" was primarily to give me as much help as they could, no matter what happened. It may have been a calculated risk on their part; but a risk calculated to give me the benefit of every doubt. It may have been Ricard's purpose to burnish their public image—for which they could have picked any one of a thousand other ways. Furthermore, no one ever asked me to wear a yellow tee-shirt with Ricard's name, or to request a glass of its product upon arriving at the finish line.

When all is said and done, my endeavor was made possible by men who had made up their minds to believe in an appealing project, one whose attraction lay perhaps in the idealism that removed it from the realm of the ordinary. And they had reached that decision in the full knowledge that they would have a lot of explaining to do to their boards of directors if, for any reason, I was unable to live up to my commitments. After all, there was nothing to guarantee that, once I was at sea, I would be willing or able to spend an hour or two a day on the radio. And there was nothing to keep me from saying that the radio was "out of order" if I wanted to take a nap.

Patrick Ricard, nonetheless, in conjunction with R.T.L., financed my truly remarkable radio equipment. This arrangement was based on a three-party agreement from which each of us would derive well-weighed advantages. (This term is deliberate: the equipment weighed almost 2,000 pounds.) I, as the navigator, would have increased security. R.T.L. would have exclusive—and, we hoped, exciting—news for its audience. And Ricard would gain stature as a public benefactor and sponsor of the adventure.

Thanks to this sponsorship, and to Credit Agricole, which was providing additional funds for repairs and renovation of the boat, *Pen Duick IV* was turned over to the Perrière shipyards in Lorient for the necessary work. Perrière, despite its impossible schedule, was the proper company to do what had to be done. After all, the boat had been built by Perrière, in 1968. It seemed the fitting place to take care of five years' wear and tear.

First, a gigantic crane plucked the trimaran from the water—it had been a rather singular sight in the fishing port—and raised it into the air like a feather, finally depositing it gently on blocks at the far end of the yard, almost at the threshold of the Tonnerre sailmakers who, of course, would also have a great deal to do with the boat's preparation.

From that time on, members of the Colas clan, battalions of them, descended upon the shipyard, while material and equipment of various kinds arrived in an apparently endless torrent. Soon, *Pen Duick IV* was little more than an aluminum carcass, stripped of all her instruments, equipment, and rigging. Dick, the Tonnerre watchdog, was delighted to have company on weekends and holidays; but I'm not sure that I can say the same for the other inhabitants of the area.

André Allègre, the architect who had designed *Pen Duick IV,* was called back from vacation in order to give his opinion, *in situ,* of the projected modifications. We quickly found that we were in agreement on the shape and the angle of the deflectors with which the stems would be equipped. And a few rather hair-raising events in past voyages, having to do with the effect of heavy seas on the stern of the boat, had given me some ideas which, to my satisfaction, coincided with those of André himself, who was very well versed in the latest developments in his profession.

These deflectors, shaped like mustaches, were intended to increase the buoyancy so as to raise the boat in the water and

17

thus, we hoped, keep it from being capsized when we encountered the giant waves of Cape Horn. The stem, streamlined to a more open angle, would break the force of the wave like the hand guard of a sword.

It was equally easy, in principle and in practice, for us to work out a fourth hull-pontoon ensemble that enveloped the forward tube. This tube itself was an addition to the original structure that had been welded amidships so as to distribute the strain when sailing against both the wind and the sea.

While we were at it, we also reduced the freeboard of the pontoons, where the impact of seawater not only created a beautiful spray effect but also acted as a brake, particularly in a crosswind.

What were the chief dangers involved in a solo voyage around the world? The first among them, of course, was the danger of being washed overboard. I knew the precautions to be taken, which consisted principally in keeping my eyes open and always being careful to have my harness hooked up.

As far as the risk of collision was concerned, it would become less and less as the course I followed deviated from the more traveled shipping lanes.

The remaining dangers were those of being dismasted and of capsizing. With respect to the former, I had stayed the two masts independently, so that, even if I lost one of them, it was unlikely that the other would also be lost. At this point in my preparations, however, my principal protection in case of capsizing lay essentially in the radio equipment that I would have aboard. There was a distress radio-buoy; all I would have to do was extend the antenna and press a button, and thereafter the radio would automatically send out an SOS, which, with luck, would be picked up by aircraft or ships within range. There was also an emergency transmitter with rabbit-ear antennas and a telescopic antenna which, if its batteries were wet, could .be activated manually by turning a handle. (The batteries, incidentally, were designed to work even if the boat were upside down.) This transmitter, enclosed in a waterproof casing, is mandatory equipment on all merchant ships. Once activated, it sends out distress signals on international MHF frequency 2182, alerting all cargo ships on that open band. This, of course, is in addition to the automatic SOS signals.

I would have enough food aboard so that, if my boat did capsize, it would become a kind of life raft that I would simply allow to drift until it reached either land or a shipping lane—that is, if my distress signals went unanswered.

To all this equipment must be added the construction of two waterproof compartments within the center hull. One of these, located aft of the boarding compartment, served to isolate the forward part of the hull. The other was to the right of the stairwell and had a waterproof door opening into the cockpit, the drainage capability of which was increased tenfold.

There were many other things as well: the use of a weatherboard on the forward hatch; the rebuilding and strengthening of the pulpits; the use of double lifelines; the installation of new tangs for modification of the rigging, of tracks for the tallboy staysail and the mizzenmast jib, of the centerboard. There was the steering system to modify, and a steering post to install under a reinforced Plexiglas dome. Actually, the installation of a sheltered steering post makes a great deal of sense from the standpoint of safety. In rough seas when the waves are washing over the decks and the boat is pitching and tossing, a helmsman under a dome has a much greater chance of pulling through than one exposed to the elements, to say nothing of the matter of comfort. There were, of course, a thousand other things—the installation of the new masts, of various keelsons, etc., etc.

Fortunately, there was no lack of experienced personnel at Lorient. The people at Perrière were not a great deal of help since a series of tests for waterproofing had revealed a number of serious weaknesses in the pontoons. We had to make large openings in the sides of the pontoons to make adjustments in the bracing but, most important, we had to redo the ten lockers which (until the tests) we had assumed to be waterproof.

These tests were, so to speak, my trump card in the preparations for my Cape Horn adventure. The (French) Atomic Energy Commission, of all people, had sent a team of specialists, headed by Roger Péclier, an engineer, to inspect the boat's aluminum struts and detect the slightest degree of porousness, weakness, and metal fatigue. (The project also served the Commission as a showcase for the techniques perfected by the safety and maintenance divisions of their installations.)

The tests themselves were quite interesting. First, the various watertight compartments were emptied of air, one by one, and the air was replaced by nitrogen. If there was the tiniest crack, or the smallest pit of corrosion through which the nitrogen leaked out of the compartment, the loss registered on a canary-yellow gauge installed on the exterior of the compartment. Ultrasonic and X-ray techniques were also used.

The X-ray tests revealed, among other things, a dangerous lack of depth in the welding of one of the joints; and the nitrogen tests, in addition to numerous leaks in the pontoons, turned up about twenty corrosion pits which had penetrated the bottom, and some leakage at the bottom of a sump—this particular discovery was something of a relief, since, for the preceding two or three years, I had had to pump out the sump every week.

Let me illustrate the value of the repairs and improvements that were made as the result of these tests. I am sailing, say, off the coast of Portugal. There is a strong wind and I am sailing closehauled. Suddenly, the forward seam of each pontoon cracks open. What do I do? Must I put into port? Not at all, since, now that the compartments are really watertight, there is no way for the water to flood them. I'll have to take it

20

easy, but I'll be able to go on, thanks to the gentlemen from the Atomic Energy Commission and their instruments.

An additional task was to try to reduce the weight of the entire structure of the trimaran as much as possible. This lightening of the structural parts had to be done mostly by cutting holes in the sides to reach the enclosed parts; and the purpose of this was to counter the (considerable) weight of the new security equipment—the radios, etc.—that was installed. Otherwise, the speed of the boat would be reduced.

In the midst of all these undertakings, a vessel that had just gone around the world, by way of the capes and through the latitudes of the forties, docked at Lorient. Loïck Fougeron, master of *Captain Brown,* had known hard times on his trip, and his weatherbeaten face and gnarled hands bore eloquent witness to his experience of the sea. There was an immediate affinity between the sailor who had just rounded the Cape, and the one who was about to round it. His ship was crammed with clever devices which he explained as I listened in fascination. Finally, he undertook a safety inspection of the trimaran. He was favorably impressed by the deflectors, but I could see that something about the boat was bothering him. And he seemed somewhat relieved when I showed him the opening that had been made in the hull for the speedometer. "Ah," he commented, "you'll be able to use that for fresh air, and for your antenna in case you capsize. But since you're still working on the boat, why don't you simply make a hatch in the bottom? You can hold it shut with wing nuts."

Loïck was right, of course, The center section of the boat had been made into a watertight living, steering, and storage area in which I would keep food, water, distress radio-buoys, batteries, and my main transmitter (which was capable of working upside-down). I had even designed a system of inflatable balloons for atop the masts. But there was no escape hatch. I had one built. If the boat capsized, all I would have to do would be to turn a few wing nuts and I would have a supply of fresh air in my compartment. Then I could calmly extend my radio antenna and send out my distress signals.

There were lists of things to be done; and lists and lists. Little by little, as the months passed, the work progressed. But the funny thing about lists is that they never grow shorter. As you cross off things at the top, you add more at the bottom. The exterior of the boat had to be treated, and both exterior and interior had to be painted. The living quarters had to be insulated and planked with wood. There were new masts (by Albert Coeudevez) to be installed. The mizzen had to have a new panel added. The mainmast had to be raised by about five feet (and thus the square footage of the sail was increased) and equipped for eight halyards, two lifts, two lines for ship's bells, and the Sarma rigging. Then, of course, there was the elaborate electrical installation to be undertaken, and the navigation aids—enough for a small cargo ship, excepting only the radar which had been banished because of the weight. I am neither Tarzan nor Superman, and I believe in supplementing muscles by such things as meteorological charts, depth-sounders, pulleys, etc.

The lists went on and on: generators, fuel tanks, heating systems, appliances, the refinishing of the upper part of the hull, the speed-regulator, the electronic equipment, the steering mechanism with its various options (a tiller in the cockpit and a wheel in the cabin), automatic pilot, manual and electric steering. There were hundreds of hours to be spent working with the people responsible for all these things and with various friends who had come to lend me a hand for a weekend and had ended by staying a month: Georges Kramabon, concealing a genius for mechanics behind a flaming red beard and an air of utter detachment; "President" de Morras, with his unquenchable enthusiasm for multihulled vessels (he was at the head of the association of owners of such boats); Albert,

Joël, Patrick, Christian, Claude, Little Louis—all caught up in the frantic pace of the work; Jeff, my kid brother, who had already been so involved in preparations for the Transatlantic, but who now, nonetheless, gave up his vacation to help ready the boat for the Cape Horn adventure. We all shared the feeling that we were racing against the clock in a madhouse of roaring compressors, blinding flashes of light from the welding equipment, clouds of dust from the dock, torrents of rain from the heavens, and the uproar from the fish auctions. Yet, throughout it all, there was a sense of warm comraderie, a companionability, that gave new meaning to the undertaking.

I must add that, beyond the technical preparations for the voyage, I also made certain, let us say, human preparations. It was not that I did not have absolute confidence in modern technology. Rather, it was more that if a man is going to fight against the elements, he has a much better chance of winning if he is in full possession of his physical and moral strength. What I wanted to do, therefore, was "humanize" the boat for those endless days when I would be alone on the sea. I felt that I would need some comfort if I was to bear the solitude (to say nothing of the danger) with patience and confidence. The human heart, if it is to remain firm, needs an occasional touch of tender, loving care.

I went over every aspect of my existence on the boat during the voyage, concentrating particularly on the comfort and attractiveness of the living quarters, the equipment in the galley, and the food to be taken. I also gave much consideration to medical supplies and pharmaceutical items necessary for my physical well-being; to the means of distracting and entertaining myself during the months of solitude; and, last but not least, to the means of protecting myself against the bitter cold I knew I would encounter.

Naturally, no one can think of everything. I was aware that it would only be at the end of the voyage that I would be in a position to draw up a definitive account of what is really needed in a galley, in radio equipment, and in each of the other areas in which I was trying to foresee everything possible to tip the odds in my favor. Hence, the innumerable treks between Lorient and Paris for supplies and equipment, the trips by air (with necktie in my pocket and a clean shirt on a coat hanger, fluttering behind me like a banner), the endless hours in automobiles, the nights on the train. Until, finally, it was all done; or, at least, as much of it as could be done. By the end of August, *Manureva* was ready for launching. *Manureva*—the name has the sound of Tahitian guitars. In the lilting language of the Polynesians, *manureva* (pronounced, man-ou-ray-va) means "bird of passage." In every boat that I had ever imagined, in every sketch of my dream boat, the name *Manureva* had appeared on the bow. Now, at the end of all the work, the modifications, the improvements, the midnight-blue trimaran, destined for the Great Capes, emerged once and for all as *Manureva*.

On pilgrimage to *Cutty Sark* at Greenwich. I wanted to immerse myself totally in the idea of sailing. (Photo Sygma)

Manureva at sunset. (Photo Jo Gauthier)

One can only imagine the peaceful splendor of the sea and the sky. (Photo A. Colas-Sygma)

My galley and my chart table. (Photos A. Colas-Sygma)

The hoisting of the "Freres de la Cote" (Coastal Brotherhood) flag when I left Sydney. I rounded the Cape under this standard. (Photo *Paris Match*-Deutsch)

The red hull of the oceanographic vessel *Endurance* is a welcome sight. *Endurance* is the rescue ship of Cape Horn. (Photo A. Colas-Sygma)

Victor Tonnerre, the master sailmaker of Lorient, France, supervises everything from the cutting of the sail to the finishing touches. Success in sailing depends largely on the care taken with the sails. (Photo Sygma)

On the dock at Lorient, my stripped-down trimaran is having its mustache-shaped deflectors installed. These deflectors are intended to keep the boat from being capsized by the gigantic waves in high latitudes. (Photo A. Colas-Sygma)

3

On course for the Cape of Good Hope

Saturday, September 8, 1973.

"Alain Colas!" The voice was like thunder and echoed against the walls. The man was like the voice. Captain "Mainmast" Gauthier, dean of the Cape Horn veterans, towered by a head over the crowd which separated before him as he made his way to the edge of the dock. He unfurled a stiff, yellowed marine chart and looked at *Manureva*.

"Alain Colas," he said again, "this chart has been used in twenty-two passages around Cape Horn, all of which ended in a safe arrival in port. I turn it over to you, with a prayer that you will bring it home safely again!"

It is impossible to describe my emotions as we cast off and *Manureva* began to move away from the crowded pier. Everyone, it seemed, had come to wish me *bon voyage,* and the dock was packed with people: my parents, their friends, my friends, people I had worked with. As the boat cleared the harbor, I thought of Dinard, on the far side of the Rance River, from which, only fifteen months before, I had left on the Transatlantic Race.

On the card table, which was to be my desk, I opened a

large red logbook and turned to page twenty-one. The last thing I had written, in a noticeably unsteady hand, was: "0015 G.M.T., across the finish-line."

I turned to the following page, as yet unmarked and, with a ruler, drew columns with the following headings: Time, Wind, Sea, Course, Log, and Comments. I added another: Thoughts. I looked at the preceding page again. Its heading was, "Plymouth to Newport." At the top of page twenty-two, after the date, I wrote: "Saint-Malo to Sydney."

God willing!

It was late afternoon and the air was gray with fog. A gust of wind sped us to the open sea. I made an entry in my log: *Time:* 1750. *Wind:* NE. *Sea:* Calm. *Course:* Steady. *Log:* 0311.79. *Comments:* Have left Saint-Malo.

By then, the boats that had formed *Manureva*'s escort out of the harbor were turning back one by one. At 1915, we had reached the level of the Vieux Banc, where the Colas clan had gathered for a last glimpse of *Manureva*. Then their silhouettes also vanished.

Well, I'm alone, I told myself. With 14,000 miles of ocean ahead of me. Instead of thinking about it, I'd better start thinking about the sails.

At 2030, we encountered a violent gale and I had to lower the mizzen. I duly noted that there were four broken battens in the mainsail—a great beginning!

By 2200, I had passed between Barnouic and Roches-Douvres, and the sea was calm again. I trimmed the mainsail and hoisted the mizzen again. My speed, at the close of this first day, was seven knots. I was satisfied.

Sunday, September 9.

I have the whole night to think about the way that lies ahead, to go over the preparations that I've made, and, I hope,

26

to comfort myself with the thought that I've done everything I can to assure that I'll be able to beat the record set by Sir Francis Chichester.

The memory of my departure from Saint-Malo is still on my mind. The old port evokes images of three-masted vessels of other times, cruising the shipping lanes under full sail. It's my intention to follow in their wakes, as it were, and to try to equal their fantastic speed. I've set a course to skirt the Canary Islands, Dakar, and the Cape Verde Islands, cross the Equator into the South Atlantic against the southeastern trade winds, and round the Cape of Good Hope. From there, *Manureva* will continue through the "roaring forties" to the Amsterdam Islands, cross the Indian Ocean, and reach Sydney by sailing between the southern tip of Australia and the island of Tasmania. Sydney, therefore, will be my first port-of-call, the end of the first leg of my journey—a distance of 14,000 miles to travel in less than three months; in less than eighty days, to be exact, if I want to beat *Cutty Sark*'s record, and in less than 106 days to beat Chichester.

Since I left on September 8, I hope to see, off Ouessant, the great sailing ships participating in the Whitbread around-the-world race organized by the British. It should be very exciting for me as I sail southward in the Atlantic to be able to test my boat and compare her performance to that of those large single-hulled vessels with their crews of no less than six. It goes without saying that these yachts—most of them of modern construction—will give a good account of themselves and that some of them will be in the next (1976) Singlehanded Transatlantic Race. I should be able to get a pretty good idea of *Manureva*'s capabilities and draw some valuable conclusions for future improvements.

The Whitbread, which is sponsored by the Royal Naval Sailing Association, is in four stages: Portsmouth to the Cape; the Cape to Sydney; Sydney to Rio de Janeiro; and Rio to

Portsmouth—a distance of some 30,000 miles. The handicaps of the participants, which are calculated for each stage, take into account length, the square footage of sail, tonnage, stability, and a number of other elements, all of which result in a "corrected time" factor. Thus, at least in theory, vessels of different sizes can compete on a basis of equality.

Since I'm going to have company on the ocean, I've compiled some information on the yachts in the race:

Burton Cutter, a British entry, is the largest, an aluminum ketch of eighty-one feet long captained by Leslie Williams, one of the stars of the 1968 Transatlantic.

Great Britain II, another British vessel, seventy-eight feet in length, is neck-and-neck with *Pen Duick VI* as the race's favorite. The captain Chay Blyth—a military man, like Tabarly—has crossed the Atlantic in a rowboat, and he also has to his credit an incredible around-the-world solo voyage without a single port-of-call. In this race, he has a crew of twelve.

Adventure, a boat belonging to the British navy, fifty-four feet long, and rigged as a sloop. The crew is composed of four teams which will relieve one another, and among the skippers are Pat Bryans and Roy Mullender.

British Soldier, a steel ketch fifty-nine feet in length, crewed by a British army team which will be changed at each port-of-call. This is the boat that, under the name *British Steel,* carried Chay Blyth around the world and that, under Brian Cook, placed fourth in the 1972 Transatlantic.

Second Life, an English ketch seventy-two feet long, crewed by a group of young men who have chartered the boat for the race. *Second Life* participated in the last Transatlantic under Gerard Djikstra, of Holland, who had sailed solo—a considerable feat, since a boat of this kind ordinarily requires a crew of from ten to fourteen.

Sayula II, a Mexican participant, was designed by Sparkman and Stephens, the famous naval architects. *Sayula II* is a

Swan 65, sixty-six feet long and rigged as a sloop. Her captain is a Mexican, Ramon Carlin; and, along with *Adventure, Sayula II* is considered an outsider in the race.

Pen Duick VI. This French entry is the last in the *Pen Duick* family, and the fruit of Eric Tabarly's experiences. She is seventy-five feet long, has an aluminum hull and 2,022 square feet of sail. Altogether a magnificent racer, designed by André Mauric.

Kriter, another French participant, is a sixty-seven foot wooden ketch. She has a French crew, and will be skippered first by Michel Malinowski, and then by Alain Glicksman.

33 Export, a French ketch, aluminum, fifty-nine feet long. Dominique Guillet and Jean-Pierre Millet are co-captains.

Grand Louis, a French schooner, sixty-one and a half feet in length. The skipper is André Viant, whose crew is composed mostly of members of his family.

Guia, an Italian sloop, is one of the smallest of the boats (along with *Copernicus*), being only forty-five and a half feet long. The captain and owner is Giorgio Falk; his alternate is Luciano Ladavas.

CS e RB (or *Koala*), an Italian boat fifty and a half feet long, of the Koala 50 series. Doi Malingri is her skipper.

Tauranga, also Italian, is a Swan 55, fifty-six feet long, with yawl rigging. Erik Pascoli is the skipper, and half the crew is Italian, half French.

Copernicus, a Polish wooden ketch, is the same length as *Guia* (forty-five and a half feet). The skipper is Polish: Zygfrid Perlicki; and he has a crew of five.

Peter von Dantzig, a German entry, was built in 1936, and is the work of the most celebrated European naval architect of that time, Henry Grüber. The skipper is Reinhard Laucht. The crew is composed of naval cadets from Kiel.

Otago, another Polish entry, is fifty-six feet in length and is the first in a series of six boats built of 4mm steel. The skipper, Zedislaw Pienkawa, has a crew of nine—one of them his daughter, and the rest shipyard employees.

Of course, I would have liked nothing better than to be a participant in the race also. But *Manureva,* with its center hull flanked by two lateral stabilizers, cannot compete on equal footing with boats of more conventional design. Then, too, I have this personal date with Cape Horn, in the middle of the second stage of the trip. I expect that I'll begin that leg of my journey from Sydney, at the end of December or the beginning of January, after a month's layover in Australia. First, south to New Zealand; then, straight for the Cape. My big moment! And also the most dangerous. Altogether, *la hora de verdad*: my moment of truth, as the bullfighters say. It will come when *Manureva* enters the narrow strait that separates the South American continent from Antarctica, where the sea seems to shrink only to gather force to punish trespassers for their insolence. After that, my course northward in the Atlantic—which will be pretty much in mid-ocean, until I cross the course I followed in the first leg of the trek—will seem simplicity itself; the straight track before a horse after the jumps of a steeplechase have been left behind.

On the second leg of my journey, also, I will be in the same area as the boats in the Whitbread Race. And, thanks to that circumstance, I will have the advantage of maximum safety—an important consideration for me. The British navy will have ships stationed in the area to keep an eye on the boats in the race. So, although I will be sailing alone, I will be surrounded by about twenty boats, all under the protective surveillance of Her Britannic Majesty's ships.

Today, Sunday, I (naturally) plotted my course about twenty times. More prosaically, I also replaced the four battens in the mainsail, broken during yesterday's blow. That, of course, was the first order of business.

30

At about 1700 hours, the sea was calm. I slackened the sails and, with the boat moving at only two knots, I went below for a nap. At 2200 hours, with the sea still calm, I took another nap. My daily routine is beginning to work itself out.

Monday, September 10.

At 0800 hours, I had my first telephone contact with shore and spoke to my elder brother, Christian.

About midday, I skirted Ouessant—a tiny island off the coast of Brittany—in dense fog but with unabated enthusiasm. Two hours later, I had my first contact with Radio-Television Luxembourg, after which I took time for a nap. When I awoke, the fog had dissipated.

I got through to my parents on the telephone. It was as though I hadn't yet left France. Several cargo ships passed on the opposite tack. I was not yet alone.

Today, I hope, was the first in a series of rather leisurely days—a period during which I'll be able to rest and recover from the months of hard work that went into preparing for the cruise.

Throughout the first night, the sky remained clear and the sea was calm. I brought my speed up to twelve knots on a course marked by a line of merchant ships. I spent several hours putting things in order in my quarters and putting the finishing touches to my rigging.

This evening, the sky was magnificent. There had been lightning earlier, but soon the moon was bright, foretelling, in my opinion, a calm sea. As it turned out, I was right. At about 0700 hours, a delicate pink sunrise confirmed my prediction.

Early Thursday morning, I rounded Cape Finisterre. Shortly thereafter, I hoisted my jib and, in the process, got thoroughly wet in a violent squall.

During the afternoon, I was in radio contact with my old friend, Roger Bouchier, a restaurant owner in Port-Saint-Germain, and then with Teura. My tour of the world was beginning with a tour of my friends.

I took a nap late in the afternoon. As soon as I awoke, I stumbled out onto the deck, still rather groggy, my eyes half-closed, to perform a perfectly natural function. I stood there, one hand grasping the railing, sleepy eyes scanning the sea, paying my tribute to Neptune. Suddenly, a short distance from *Manureva*—perhaps 200 yards away—I saw a movement in the water. I looked more closely, this time with my eyes wide open. It appeared to be a long, black tube of some kind, rising slowly to the surface. The tube was emitting a rush of bubbles and I had the distinct feeling that it was *looking* at me. I quickly finished what I was doing and beat a hasty retreat. It was not until I was in my quarters that I was able calmly to identify this black object that looked like the arm of a giant squid poised to strike. It was the air hose of a submarine coming to the surface.

When you're half asleep, the sight of something long and black rising to the surface in a geyser of bubbles tends to awaken atavistic memories of sea serpents. I confess that I am not particularly proud of my reaction. However, my visitor seemed to be as surprised as I was by this unexpected encounter and, after a few moments of hesitation, the "head" submerged and, trailing a stream of bubbles, it slowly disappeared into the distance.

Friday, September 14.

A small misadventure during the night: the boat was hit by a large wave, and my quarters were flooded by a rush of water through the air vent.

Before dawn, I sighted a couple of boats on the other tack.

The sea began to get rough around noon. It was worse than ever when, at 1700, I sighted a sloop. She was close enough for me to make out the number on her sail: I.4971. It was Giorgio Falk's *Guia,* one of the Italian entries in the Whitbread, closehauled in a brisk wind from the southeast. The *Guia* was using her jib with her mainsail reefed. I decided to tack and test *Manureva*'s performance—under full sail, from mizzen to main—against the Italian boat. With new sails and new rigging, one doesn't take chances; and it seemed to me better to find out what, if anything, might be wrong before we reached the roaring forties.

Soon, *Manureva* was abreast *Guia,* and we were exchanging hand signals. I was proud of the way *Manureva* was handling herself, cutting through the waves, glistening with spray in the orange light of an evening squall. Both boats were holding to the same course, but I was doing about two knots better than *Guia.* I pulled ahead, and the gap began to widen. Soon, I was about a mile ahead of the Italians. And then we were too far apart for hand signals.

I heard, on the radio, that *Kriter* was off the coast of Lisbon, ahead of *Grand Louis. Adventure* was in the lead, but only by about thirty-five miles.

Saturday, September 15.

I spent the whole morning tacking and, at the same time, doing as much as I could of my various chores: adjusting the stays, repairing a broken slide on the mainsail, etc. I also made a note of the first repairs to be made as soon as I reached Sydney: mend the backstays on the mainmast; modify the spinnaker downhaul; work on the winches.

By early afternoon, I was abreast of the mouth of the Tagus River.

Toward dusk, I was hailed (rather loudly) by the tanker *Jules Verne,* out of Le Havre.

By then, I was tired, and I set the self-steerer so that I could take a nap. This device—also known as an automatic pilot and (more accurately) as a direction and speed anemometer—serves to keep the boat on a proper course in relation to the wind. Part of the mechanism is installed aloft in the direction of the wind and, if the boat deviates from her course, a corrected course is transmitted from the aerial to a submerged element and the deviation is rectified, theoretically, at least.

I awoke around 2100 hours. The moon had risen while I slept, and, in the distance, I could see Lisbon bathed in silvery light. It was a somewhat eerie spectacle, like a vision of an enchanted city; and I celebrated the event by a banquet of sliced cooked meat, home-style.

I have already been at sea for a week, and it is time for me to draw up my accounts. From the time of my departure, I have sailed 848 nautical miles between meridian points. A record! But it is a record for slowness, considering how long the boat has been in the water! I must admit that, for the first few days, I have been much more concerned with getting proper rest than with speed. Exhausted as I was by the preparations for the voyage, and by the panic of the final days, I've been treating myself to relatively long periods of sleep; and I've also spent time working in my quarters so that I can feel at home as much as possible. It takes time to get over eight months of unremitting work and stress. Now I'm going to have to make up for lost time. Nonetheless, I'm not too disturbed. Everything seems to have fallen into place, and *Manureva* has found her own rhythm. Closehauled, she pulled ahead of *Guia;* and, generally speaking, closehauled sailing is the least favorable trim for a trimaran. This has, if anything, increased my confidence in the boat. I haven't the slightest doubt that, when the moment of truth comes, both the captain and the ship will be in tiptop shape to handle anything that comes along.

If there is a fly in the ointment, it is this: there are cracks at the spot where the forward cross bar is joined to the floats. I will have to ease up a bit when closehauled, because the deflectors and the other gear on the bow, installed with a view to the wind on the quarter, put a strain on this area. Fortunately, the Atomic Energy Commission's tests made it possible for me to insure that the compartments in the floats are really watertight. Any leaks will be limited to the forward compartment and, even there, the expanded foam will lessen the problem. As far as the masts are concerned, the tests were conclusive. Now that the sea is calm again, I am going to adjust the middle guys of the mainmast rigging to bend the mast—contrary to house rules.

It is midnight, and we are becalmed.

Sunday, September 16.

I was up on the bridge at 0500 and saw that a current of some kind had carried me past Lisbon. I could not even see the lights of the city.

Today is my birthday. I have reached my thirtieth year off the coast of Portugal. The sea did not forget me. As a present, I received a beautiful flying fish, about the size of a large mackerel, which landed on the deck. I will have it for lunch. It would be improper for me to refuse the gift.

I unwrapped my other presents, given by family and friends before I sailed from Saint-Malo. Some chocolate. A selection of my favorite delicacies. A book. A small, light green skirt. A skirt? I folded and unfolded it in puzzlement. A joke? A mistake? A sign of some kind? I had no idea. It was incontestably a skirt; and a very small one. And it was undoubtedly a present—giftwrapping, ribbons, bows. Then I remembered. My niece from Dinard had been aboard, and Teura or Mamy had given her a gift. She had left it in the cabin. I was greatly relieved.

I made a note: "Adjust the swifter and give the backstay three turns. Modify the main sheet."

At 1400, my parents wished me happy birthday via radiotelephone.

According to Radio-Luxembourg, *Pen Duick VI* is already between Madeira and Morocco, and *Adventure* is some 200 miles behind her.

At about 1900, I had a set of excellent weather maps on *Manureva*'s facsimile receiver, a piece of equipment that does a great deal for safe navigation. With a receiver of this kind, there is almost no such thing as an unexpected storm. The maps, showing every depression in the area, are drawn as though by magic on a roll of kaolin paper by a set of styluses activated by distant signals.

It is 2100, and the sea is still calm. The speed-regulator is pulling too much to the left and I have to take it down. I will use the automatic electric pilot system.

Monday, September 17.

I began the day by an act of outrageous self-indulgence: that is, I took three hours of sound sleep, between 0630 and 0930.

The sky is gray and depressing. I kept busy by getting ready for my radio contact with R.T.L., scheduled for 1100 hours. Reception is excellent. The first news was of the race. *Pen Duick VI* is leading and is off the coast of Casablanca, with *Great Britain* trailing her by 100 miles.

I announced my position: 36°10'N and 10°20'W, about

level with Gibraltar. A cooperative little wind was enabling me to make good time southward, and I hoped to be able to make up for lost time.

I went on to tell about my week, lingering a while over the story of my encounter with the submarine. My correspondent seemed amused. I then explained that Tabarly's lead in the Whitbread Race was to be expected. He was a demon for speed and, after all, large boats do tend to go fast.

"As far as I myself am concerned," I went on, "I'm going to try to make up for lost time. However, I am the only person aboard *Manureva*—and you have to remember that the boats in the race each have an average of twelve crewmen. While I'm sleeping, for instance, the boat is left pretty much on her own; there's no one on deck to take advantage of every favorable breeze or gust that comes along. My problem is the wind. When there is wind, *Manureva* holds to her course very nicely on automatic pilot; but when the wind is weak, or variable, she tends to wander. I'd have to be at the helm twenty-four hours a day to keep her steady; and that, obviously, is impossible. However, I expect that I'll be able to make up for it when I get a bit farther south, where I'll certainly find the trade winds, which are fairly constant and sustained out of the northeast."

Listening to myself, it occurred to me that the closer I got to Sydney, the more I sounded like a professor giving a lecture.

My interviewer seemed concerned about my solitude. He asked if time were heavy on my hands. Like most people, he felt that a man sitting in a boat and waiting for the trade winds must be bored out of his mind. "Absolutely not," I answered. "You'll never believe how much there is to do aboard when you're all alone. You have to spend a great deal of time at the helm, in the galley, or tacking, navigating, puttering around, keeping everything ship-shape, and so forth. I have at least two weeks of work ahead of me right now, just getting everything in order.

"I listen to music a great deal. And I listen to the news more than I used to. The reason, no doubt, is that I am slowing down in my old age, having turned thirty only yesterday.''

I also confessed that, in an orgy of egocentricity, I had listened to Radio-Luxembourg constantly during the past week, hoping to hear the sound of my own voice. The interviewer seemed surprised that I could still get his station. Whereupon, I felt it only fair to remind him that there were other stations on the air as well. Finally, I was assured that I had missed nothing; that my broadcasts were scheduled to begin on Wednesday.

My radio contact with France was excellent, and I was delighted to have it.

Early in the afternoon, I rigged my gennikers, which are balloonlike jibs, on a telescopic boom. This made me miss a radio date with *33 Export,* one of the boats in the race that is crewed by friends of mine. I had reached them yesterday, and we chatted for a long time on ship-to-ship radio. They have minor problems also, and work to do; but everything seems to be going well enough.

I'm sorry I missed talking to them today, although I can't spend all my time on the radio. I wanted to talk to them, not only because they're friends, but also because I am very interested in finding out whether or not I am gaining on them, making up for some of the time I lost during my slow crossing of the Bay of Biscay.

During the afternoon, the relative calm of the sea made it possible for me to take time out for a number of chores: I made a weather map, adjusted the exhausts on the head, rearranged the sail bins, and so forth. I ended the day—a peaceful day, but busy—with a solid meal.

Tuesday, September 18.

I awoke during the night to find *Manureva* lying to and falling astern at four or five knots. I immediately hauled down the miz-

38

zen and the mainsail, hoisted one of my big gennikers, and we were soon moving forward again. But that was not quite as easy as it sounds. There was a lift caught in the wrong place and I had to do a trapeze number in order to free it.

The days are getting somewhat long. Still, since passing Gibralter, the winds have been from the northeast, and *Manureva* is flying along with her two white wings forward. No one, unless he has done it, can know quite what it means to handle two sails at once, each with an area of about 400 square feet. But I kept reminding myself that, after the Cape Horn adventure, there was the 1976 Transatlantic coming up. And for that I would have to be an expert. The future, I expect, belongs to the boats with the largest sails. So, there is nothing to do but get ready to convert the rigging; and, meanwhile, to polish techniques with telescopic booms.

33 Export is now sixty miles south of Madeira.

This is the seventh night at sea for *Manureva* and me. I can see the lights of Allegranza, on Fuerteventura (the most easterly of the Canary Islands). The trade winds are blowing, and I am being particularly cautious because of the darkness; not that the darkness itself is especially hazardous, but the Eastern Rock lies near the course that I've charted for *Manureva* between the Canaries and the coast of Morocco. The lights of Allegranza are very faint. I can hardly make them out. They will be lost entirely by the time we reach the Rock—although my imagination sees it right now in the shape of almost every wave.

I went below from time to time to check the sounding apparatus which, when I turn a switch, uses a stylus to trace the profile of the bottom. I watched the stylus move. Then, suddenly, my heart skipped a beat. The stylus had leaped to the top of the paper. I raced to the helm and leaned on it with all my weight while my eyes tried to pierce the darkness around me. At last, I saw the Rock, rising somberly out of the sea, safely to starboard. I cannot say how far away it was, since it is difficult to estimate in the darkness. But one thing is certain: even if it does nothing else, the sounding apparatus has already justified its existence.

It is 0420 hours, and we are in deep water again. Serenity is restored aboard *Manureva* as I watch the Rock recede in the night.

Wednesday, September 19.

I established contact with R.T.L. at 1000, and with *Tintin* at 1100. I have promised to send regular radio-telegrams to *Tintin* for the sake of their young readers, and, once I reach port in Australia, to send photographs. What I had to do was to prepare a broadcast for radio listeners; and then, one hour later, transmit the same news—but this time in language intelligible to children. It is not an easy job; but I take pleasure in sharing with other people what I am experiencing and what I am seeing on the ocean.

I heard this morning that *Pen Duick VI* is within sight of the Canary Islands. *Great Britain* is still trailing her, but now at a distance of 100 miles.

I was in contact with *33 Export* at 1400 hours. Then I spent the rest of the afternoon putting things in order in the aft compartment.

I slept like a log for two hours, between 1800 and 2000 hours, in anticipation of staying awake most of the night because we were approaching Cape Bojador.* I will have to keep an eye on the weather maps. But I am very tired. I haven't slept more than a few hours for the past three nights.

---

*On the northwest coast of Africa.

Thursday, September 20.

At three o'clock this morning I was almost asleep on my feet. Finally, at 0630 I was able to get three hours of rest. During the morning, I altered the halyards and lifts to keep the steel cables from fraying.

The Atlantic seems crowded today. I passed a fleet of fishing boats going in the opposite direction. And, following the same course, *Saloroman* out of Huelva. An hour later, we encountered *Ever Reliance,* a cargo ship, whose name, for some reason, is repeated in Chinese characters.

I was not able to establish radio contact with *33 Export* this afternoon.

I hooked up the short-wave receiver and the time signal. For days, I had been trying to summon up enough courage to undertake the intricate wiring job that this involves.

This evening, I was surprised to hear myself singing out loud for the first time this trip.

This is my twelfth day at sea; and I am, at this moment, subjected to the full magic of a tropic night as I linger at the helm, feeling the time slip by. It has been a rather long day, much of it spent watching the trawlers working the continental shelf.

The three hours of sleep that I snatched this morning are standing me in good stead. I am able somehow to keep my eyes open, and my mind reasonably alert, despite the fact that I will soon have been on watch for seventy-two hours. The watch is necessary, of course, because of the rather peculiar way that I charted my course between the Canary Islands and the Moroccan coast, so that, later, I can cut the distance along Rio de Oro and Mauritania.

I am now in more or less regular contact with *33 Export,* thanks to Dominique Guillet's efforts. Dominique arranged the contact with Saint-Lys Radio, the wireless service for ships at sea, in order to tear me from my splendid isolation.

With the news of the Whitbread Race coming in regularly, I now feel that I have plenty of company in the South Atlantic. My racing instinct nudges me daily, and I make a habit of evaluating the chances of each boat on the basis of how far ahead or how far behind each one is in relation to the others.

I have just taken a reading on the depth sounder: 1,078.

There are fishing boats everywhere around here.

Friday, September 21.

Villa Cisneros is nearby, according to the radio; and I have just sighted a mail plane. I have been trying, unsuccessfully, to pick up a weather report from Port-Etienne (called Nuadibu, nowadays) in Mauritania.

One day follows another and they are all alike. Early in the afternoon, under lowering skies, I crossed the Tropic of Cancer. The trade winds are blowing stronger.

Handling the telescopic booms has become a matter of routine, and it seems to me that I am making up some of the time I lost earlier.

On the opposite tack: *World Victoria,* a tanker; then, several freighters.

My watch goes on.

Saturday, September 22.

There were a number of flying fish on deck this morning, the making of a small banquet.

Near noon, the wind suddenly shifted to the east. The water here is alive with fish, and birds are wheeling overhead. Is there something special about this spot?

I am at the end of my second week and I have drawn up a balance sheet. I confess that I knew beforehand that the results would be positive; and I was not disappointed: 1,335 miles. We are on the right track.

33 Export is now only eight miles ahead of *Manureva*. I also picked up *Adventure* this morning, as well as several other boats, and chatted with them for a while. I have noted their positions in my log.

Sunday, September 23.

Today, the sea is wearing her Sunday-best of indigo under a sun which cuts through the clouds accompanying the trade winds: the "phosphorescent blue of the tropic seas," as they say. A squadron of joyous flying fish accompanies *Manureva* as she glides through the water at her customary nine knots.

I am celebrating Sunday by relaxing. There were a few chores, of course, which I performed after spending time in an attentive reading of Sir Francis Chichester's account of his voyage. Now, on the first leg of my journey, it seems to me that it's essential to read such things in order to be able to sense, beyond the words themselves, the day-to-day reality.

This morning's weather report from Dakar was encouraging, and the forecast is favorable. I spent some time trying, on the basis of the information I have, to determine the general positions of the participants in the Whitbread. Last night, the B.B.C. and the O.R.T.F. gave *Pen Duick VI* first place and *33 Export* second (I have the latter's position: 13°50′N, 23°00′W). Then come *Kriter, Koala F3* (her official name is CS e RB) and *Guia*. It gives me a strange feeling to watch the dots representing these boats progress across my map, and I remind myself that the dots are the sum of the work and the will of other men.

Monday, September 24.

I managed to stay awake all night, thanks to the bright stars and the moonlight. Also, it's less hot at night than during the day.

I had some good radio contacts during the day: the weather report from Dakar, a broadcast from Paris, a conversation with *33 Export,* and so forth. *33 Export* is sailing squarely through the Cape Verde archipelago and is now a few gusts of wind into the islands. At the moment, we are at the same latitude; and we are both suffering through the same heat. Aboard *Manureva,* it is 99°F in the shade. There is lots of news from Radio-Dakar—weather reports, commentaries on the Whitbread Race, etc. Since my radio break in the morning is not long enough for everything, I also now have a radio break during the afternoon.

These radio contacts have gradually become pivotal points around which my days revolve, along with the dawn and the sunset, the rhythm of meals, and of course the sacred hour of noon, when a seaman salutes the sun with his sextant to establish his position.

Pen Duick VI is now some 400 miles south of the islands.

Before nightfall, I ran up the mizzen and the mainsail, brought in a genniker and got a spinnaker ready; all of which constitutes the evening toilette of *Manureva* and makes her more maneuverable in case of unexpected bad weather. Then I took up my post next to the radio, listening for the latest news of the race from the B.B.C.

Tuesday, September 25.

During the night there was lightning on the horizon, probably announcing a tropical front and, behind that front, the equatorial calm of the Doldrums—an area where thick clouds and heavy rains abound.

Early in the afternoon I heard that *33 Export* had gained thirty miles on me, and *Kriter*—I talked with them this morning—twenty miles. I had better start shaping up!

I hoisted my staysail and we took off. At midnight a school of dolphins came alongside to play.

Wednesday, September 26.

This is my eighteenth day at sea, and I am exactly midway between the Cape Verde Islands and the Equator. Between the Canaries and the Cape Verde Islands, I relaxed and took it easy. The boat handled herself and I took long naps between my daily chores. I was able to do this because I was now out of the shipping lanes used by freighters, trawlers, and cruising vessels. Once I passed Dakar, I was alone on the ocean and able to get several good nights of sleep. I now feel in tiptop shape and I think I've recovered completely from the accumulated fatigue of preparing for the journey.

I am still reading Chichester.

I am about to enter that stretch of absolute calm alternating with violent squalls, known to mariners as the *Pot au Noir,* or Doldrums. It is a name that evokes the memory of great sailing ships becalmed for weeks on end, their sails hanging limp from the masts, and then leaping ahead under the impulse of a sudden apocalyptic blow strong enough to rip the clothes from a man's back and wet enough to pass for a waterfall rather than a rain.

The area is about 300 miles wide running from west to east, beginning at 5°N and widening as it nears the African coast at 20°W. Normally, trade winds from the northeast carry boats from the Canary Islands to this area, which is the first difficult

45

stretch of navigation to be encountered. Then the trade winds are normally from the southeast. At that point, a boat sails as close into the wind as possible—while making sure to avoid the high pressure area of the South Atlantic where the wind is also usually remarkable for its absence.

From there, there are two possible strategies. Either give the high pressure area as wide a berth as possible by going far to the west and compensating for this extra distance by going far enough south to reach the strong winds of the "roaring forties." Or, sail directly into the southeast trade wind and skirt around the high on the east side. In the latter case, you run the risk of several days of total calm, which are compensated for, to some extent, by the glorious sun in this high pressure area.

In any case, for the moment the sky ahead of *Manureva* is dark with clouds; and they soon appear alongside as well. There is no doubt that I am heading into the Doldrums. The humidity is stifling, and the wind is slacking.

We are in the first squall.

It has been followed by a dead calm.

Squall follows squall and the black clouds erupt into torrents. Then, the sea is absolutely flat for a while, until we are hit with sudden violent gusts. These unpredictable changes naturally require that I remain at the helm, and I am constantly tacking to keep in the right direction in the shifting wind. There's no doubt that I'm going to my equatorial crossing this time.

At sunset the sky is the color of ink. My work at the helm is now less demanding. Sunset and sunrise are the only moments of relief from the long, hot days. I yearn for a spell of cool air and a few hours of relaxation.

My friendly dolphins are with me now, cutting like torpedoes through the swell. There are thousands of insects— flies, butterflies, dragonflies—no doubt blown here from the African coast.

Thursday, September 27.

Throughout the night there were squalls on the horizon and stars overhead. In the morning: several heavy rains, one of which drenched both the cabin and the captain.

By evening, the wind was from the south and the clouds were white, like great balls of diaphanous cotton scattered in well-ordered ranks. The danger zone was behind us, and the South Atlantic lay before *Manureva*'s bow.

I had excellent radio contact with R.T.L. yesterday at noon, and I was able to give a good account of myself. In the second week, we covered almost 1,400 miles; which means that we've made up for most of the low average of the first few days. *Manureva* and I are now well within Chichester's record; in fact, we have four days on his itinerary—which is particularly encouraging, for Chichester had good strong winds from the very beginning and he was able to move quite fast. In my broadcast, I tried to convey something of the poetry of this passage through the magnificent trade wind weather, talking about the cumulus clouds in their neat rows, the deep water pulsing with life, the flashes of color as the flying fish leap from the sea. I also told the audience about an incident that occurred last night aboard *Kriter*—an incident that could easily have had a tragic ending. During a maneuver, the spinnaker sheet lashed out of control, knocking one of the crewmen overboard. Fortunately, he was able to grab hold of the sheet as he went over. It was a very dark night, and it was only by luck that his shipmates saw him after he had been towed through the water for several endless minutes.

There is something to learn from this accident. The crewman obviously was not wearing his safety harness. That sometimes happens. A sudden squall comes up and you must rush up on deck before things get out of hand. You're not willing to take the time—or you can't take the time—to buckle yourself in. The elements simply do not wait for a man to do what he is supposed to do. And that is how accidents happen. Even so, the experience aboard *Kriter* is in the nature of a warning. Everyone needs such warnings from time to time; and I more than most people.

Finally, I talked about my course and we exchanged various bits of news. I am now in daily contact with a half-dozen sailing vessels moving like a convoy. According to my calculations, these are their actual positions: shortly, *Pen Duick VI* will be in the lead by a comfortable margin, followed by a Mexican entry, *Sayula,* which is almost neck-and-neck with *Great Britain.* Then come *Kriter, 33 Export,* and *Manureva*—our positions at any given time depending on whether I move up on them or they pull ahead of me.

Obviously, the range of the naked eye from a boat like mine is probably no more than five miles, and so I cannot see any of my friends. (I'm so involved in the race that I almost wrote "my competitors.") I'll therefore have to wait for my radio breaks to know who's gaining on whom and who is where.

R.T.L. gives me the positions of the boats in corrected time, computed on the basis of information organized by the race committee. There has been a change since yesterday. *Pen Duick VI* is no longer in the lead; and, in corrected time, the positions are as follows: first, *CS e RB;* second, *Guia;* third, *Pen Duick VI;* fourth, *Kriter;* fifth, *Adventure;* sixth, *33 Export;* seventh, *British Soldier.*

During my radio contact with R.T.L., I sent various personal messages: news to my family; a request that the Maritime Radio Company (C.R.M.) send me, via Saint-Lys Radio, copies of the Pretoria weather forecasts, areas covered by the different bulletins, and so forth. My contact at the other end was not sure he understood what I wanted—I can't blame him—and he said that he would send C.R.M. a copy of the tape, so that I'd be sure of getting what I asked for. We may use sails the way our grandfathers did, but we still make sure that we take advantage of the technical skills of our own time.

Thus far, all the news is good. The latest charts have arrived from London and will be turned over to my family, to be delivered to me in Sydney. My films are practically all sold and money is trickling in. The more miles of ocean we cover, the tighter seem the bonds that bind us to our friends. My daily radio contacts with the other boats have a very positive effect on my morale. I may be a hermit by inclination, but I do like to know that there is something around me other than the sea.

Friday, September 28.

There was a small but troublesome squall during the night.

At 0800 hours, I discovered that *Manureva* was heading *north* and was not having an easy time against the squalls that seem to come from every direction. Contrary to what I believed, I am obviously not out of the Doldrums. Or perhaps I'm in a second phase of it. I'm keeping an ear on the frequencies that will put me in contact with *Grand Louis* and perhaps with *Pen Duick VI*. My position now is 5°15′N, 21°40′W. I spent the entire afternoon at the helm in a disagreeable little drizzle. There is a solid swell from the south, a sign of wind in the distance.

The night consoled me for the afternoon: lightning in the distance, but stars overhead.

Saturday, September 29.

The night passed slowly and I made many entries in the log—chiefly: "came about" and "jibed."

The sky was gray at dawn and remained gray throughout the forenoon. The squalls never stopped. My position is 4°12′N.

49

There was another squall during the afternoon.

A slice of life from land: I talked to my parents at 2100 hours.

Looking back on my third week at sea, I have every reason to be pleased. This week's 1,211 miles, added to the first two weeks, total 3,394 miles since leaving Saint-Malo. Today's entry in the log ends with these words: "God willing, I'll continue to do as well in the weeks to come."

This morning, I heard that *Pen Duick VI* had crossed the Equator. *Kriter* is next (she's now at 2°22'N), then *33 Export* (2°31'N), while *Guia* (5°30'N) has just emerged from calm water.

The next week was spent following the good old day-to-day routine of any sailor at sea.

I was in radio contact with R.T.L. several times but was unable to make any decent tapes because the sound kept fading in and out. I yelled myself hoarse trying to give an intelligible account of what had happened aboard: a description of the damp, somber Doldrums; the squalls; my hands constantly so wet that my calluses fell off; the mildewed bread that I had to dry out in the sun and then cut with a hacksaw because it was so hard that an ordinary knife couldn't get through it.

The race is as exciting as ever, and I'm kept busy transcribing the respective positions of the participants in my radio log. I would not be doing badly at all if I were in the race. Naturally, everyone is trying as hard as he can; but it seemed that the tide had definitely turned in favor of *Pen Duick VI*, until the news came that the large ketch had lost her mast only 1,800 miles from the finish line and would have to put into Rio. Aside from the possibility of injuries, losing a mast is a very serious business—a sudden ripping apart of stays, spars, sails, and rigging. On a large sailing vessel, the aluminum mast is over seventy-five feet high and weighs nearly a ton.

When it goes, it and its rigging and its thousands of square feet of sail fall across the deck where the crew is trying to maneuver. A dismasting occurs usually when there is a heavy blow and when the boat is sailing upwind. And, since all racing boats everywhere are always pushing to the maximum degree, it sometimes happens that one of the links of the chain that constitutes a sailing vessel breaks. Then we have a catastrophe. A dismasting, no doubt, is part of the "law of the sea," having to do with imponderables and with an element of "chance." Even so, I hope that no one was hurt. We're all in the same boat, in a sense, and I feel a very personal involvement in the dismasting of *Pen Duick VI*.

I've had a few small problems of my own because, like everyone else, I feel a very strong temptation to push *Manureva* as hard as possible in search of optimum performance.

One morning, I was struggling with a large foresail that gives me ten to twelve knots of speed. Suddenly, the rigging broke; and there I was, trying to handle 236 square feet of sail suddenly gone crazy. An interesting game.

It was a sign, and a sign that could not be mistaken. When a wire rope, which has been load-tested at 1.5 tons, breaks in a gale, it means that you are well advised to reduce your speed. It is like a wink from a guardian angel. I understood it as such and reduced sail accordingly.

The following day, I was able to get news over the radio about Eric Tabarly's mast. For reasons unknown, the mast had simply folded over. The shrouds were cut, and the mast and sails went overboard. Albert Coeudevez, at Espar Nirvana, in France, was now undertaking the impossible: he had promised to have a new mast ready in five days. It would be flown to Rio, to be installed on *Pen Duick VI*.

I took down several telegrams from *33 Export* to relay by way of Saint-Lys. There's no doubt that my elaborate radio equipment is justifying its existence. Of course, I am delighted to be able to reach France and even Great Britain. The next day, Saint-Lys confirmed receipt of the messages and passed on a telegram from *Pen Duick VI:* "No one hurt and morale high."

My week on the radio ended with a very clear communication with Clamecy, France, where my whole family was waiting. My brother Jeff began giving me all the news. A few excerpts will give an idea of the highly technical level of our exchanges: "George says to tell you that the Modulog needles should be in the racks above the chart table. . . . And don't worry about the bottles of Evian and the paint. They'll be in Sydney when you get there. . . . About the oil: It should be at about 45; and don't let it go below 20. . . . The acetometer should read 1250 at the end of the charge; so you're going to have to recharge the batteries when it goes down to 1200. Do it as soon as possible, because you're using your radio a lot. And let it charge for four or five hours at a time."

I didn't know quite how to explain that my acetometer was made in Japan, and that it had colors instead of numbers.

"I'm doing OK with the fuel," I assured Jeff. "My generator is using only about a quart and a half per hour, and I have about 106 gallons on hand." (I had kept careful notes, in my log, of how much fuel the generator was using over a given period of time.)

We then talked about *Pen Duick VI*'s mishap, and Jeff confirmed what I had heard, that Albert Coeudevez expected to have the new mast ready the following Tuesday. Victor Tonnerre, meanwhile, was making a new mainsail, a fore-staysail, and a staysail.

If they can do it, they'll deserve the gratitude of everyone concerned.

Everything was going well at home, and everyone was there for vacation: my parents, my nephew Alexander who, according to Pierrette, wakes up every morning shouting, "Good luck, Colas!"

"Ask Albert Coeudevez about modifying the binding on the mainmast," I told Jeff. The accident aboard *Pen Duick VI* had made me think about reinforcing the masts by rerigging the extra shrouds. I was thinking especially about the strain on the mast in case of very strong trailing winds. But I wanted Albert's opinion before I decided anything.

The rest of the conversation was about domestic matters, and it ended with the usual string of how-are-you's and we-miss-you's. Even those hackneyed formulas are sweet to the ear of a man who is alone. "*Bon voyage,*" Jeff concluded. "We're all thinking of you, and we all send our love. So long!"

These gusts of warmth and affection, it seemed to me, rose up and joined together above the land and the water and made me think of the "vast birds of the sea" that the poets write about. I was touched and comforted, and I was in good humor when I sat down to compute my progress for the fourth week: 1,201 miles, between meridian points. Unless I have made a mistake somewhere, my average speed has risen to seven knots, for an average of 164 miles a day.

I am still keeping track of the amount of fuel that my generator is using. The generator has operated a total of seventy hours since I left Saint-Malo and has used twenty-eight gallons of the gas-oil mixture. Therefore, I have about seventy-nine gallons left; which is to say 100 days' use, if I use the generator an average of two hours a day.

Since there have been so few problems lately, I've managed to get two successive nights of good sleep. These are the first since setting sail. But the Alain Colas who is buried in my subconscious mind apparently does not like such innovations. I woke up once at 0300, thinking I heard someone calling me by name.

I've also had time for some enjoyable reading: documents on the Sydney-bound clippers (*Patriarch, Cutty Sark, Cimba, Samuel Plimsoll, Rodney*); and a couple of enjoyable days spent in the literary company of Captain Voss. After that, I turned to *Strange Stories of the Sea* for a bit of relaxation, but was disappointed. I switched to Olivier Stern-Veyrin, and this time I was not at all disappointed.

I am also trying to vary my pleasures. For example, I am spending a good deal of time preparing worthwhile meals. On occasion, I even verge on the exotic by preparing Chinese food. I've begun to dig into my canned goods, and I've even opened a box of ravioli, a sure sign that I've been at sea for a while.

Wednesday, I had to break open a dozen eggs to find three good ones.

I was about to forget the big day. On Monday, October 1, at 1721 hours, I crossed the Equator at 24°34'W. Somehow, although I studied the horizon carefully, I was not able to find any evidence of that lovely black line that was nonetheless shown on all the big colored globes when I was a schoolboy. I halfway expected Neptune to rise from the depths, triton in hand, and come aboard to observe the appropriate formalities of the crossing. Perhaps he has grown accustomed to me. After all, this is the sixth time I have crossed the line.

I must say that I am pleased with the way things are going. The five tall ships that, to my knowledge, reached Sydney in the record time of seventy-two days, had all taken between twenty-one and twenty-six days to reach the Equator. It took Chichester twenty-six days. My time was twenty-two and a half days.

To tell the truth, things have not always gone smoothly. There have been days of slack wind when we crept along at a few knots, and even that only by pushing as hard as we could. There have been little malfunctions that take time and trouble. My list of minor repairs to be taken care of at Sydney is beginning to grow: change the halyards on the jib and mizzen; think about using two lateral shrouds and talk to Albert about the mast; install safety-hanks on the jib; change the hanks on the staysail; check in Sydney to see about the halyards.

There is nothing serious on the list. And, after all, the important thing is to keep nibbling away at the miles. Everything else is a detail.

The relative calm during this past week gave me time to think about myself; and, as it happens every time I am at sea, a series of questions has been whirling around in my head, looking for answers. This record-setting trek, for instance: this need to go faster in order to achieve a passing and fragile victory—what does it amount to?

Now, alone at the Equator, I am searching my mind; not only to find answers, but also to make certain that I am not trying to evade the real questions. Of course, I do not expect a sudden illumination of my deepest motivations in one day of reflection or in one week; certainly not at the very moment I succeed in formulating a question. I've already spent a number of years questioning the sea, and I count myself lucky if, in all these thousands of miles, I have enjoyed a few passing moments of understanding.

I have known the joy of rising above what I thought were my own limits. But why do some people love battle and others prefer retreat? Why do some prefer participation with others, while some can be content only when they have imposed their own will on others? Why do some people leave, and others stay, in order to find themselves? We say, with a smile, that we want to prove ourselves, to have our chance. But are we actually motivated by wounded pride?

Pride, certainly, has a lot to do with it. There is occasion for great pride when we experience a victory that we have earned for ourselves with our own hands. But then, aren't we forgetting that we are merely the standard-bearers of all those who have given the best of themselves at every step of the way in preparing the boat for the journey?

There are many elements that make up a victory, and the

human element is not the dominant one. In the final analysis, I know very well that a victory over the sea is not "won" through a struggle. It is given by default, as it were; and the true master of the situation remains, as always, the sea itself.

The world of sailing is so vast that there is room in it for everyone and everything. You have, on the one hand, the pure, austere discipline of the solitary sailor at sea; and, on the other, you have the Sunday sailor, his little craft riding gently at anchor in the snug harbor of a sheltered bay. What do these two have in common, except the basic rhythms of that art? Who would dare attempt to establish a hierarchy of sailing? Who can say that the man alone in his dinghy on a quiet lake gathers less wealth from his boat, or finds fewer ways of expressing himself, than the crewmen working shoulder to shoulder in the virile comraderie of a transoceanic race?

The very idea of being "better" should be alien to the sailor; as alien as the idea of a piano virtuoso that he should be the sole and unique interpreter of this or that composer. In both cases, it is a matter of serving something that is greater than the individual, of being one interpreter of music or, as I am perhaps, one interpreter of the harmony of the seas. To put it more simply, perhaps we should think only of a certain lifestyle, of a certain mode of existence. Not of *being* the best, but of *doing* our best. No doubt, doing our best implies a desire to excel; but, more than that, it also implies a desire to better ourselves. In any case, it should mean that, within myself, I want to be a better Alain Colas. At the risk of sounding professorial again, I must go on to say that I am more concerned with exploring the meaning of myself than I am with exploring the meaning of sailing. But, in order to do that, I realize that I must perceive myself, observe myself, in action; that is, in a situation of self-betterment.

On the sea and through the sea, I've discovered that I have a love of discovery, regardless of where it may lead. For that reason, I believe that in their intensity, in their human context, preparations for such undertakings as the Transatlantic Race or rounding Cape Horn are extremely effective in bringing one to a proper perception of oneself as a developing person. The links of comraderie and friendship that are forged in the common tension of such preparations make us see ourselves as we are, deep within ourselves. And the technical and technological skills that are exhibited lead us to appreciate the homogeneity of humanity and, at the same time, the necessity for diversity of skills and talents.

My greatest pleasure is in learning. For me, it is the richest reward. I have always hated being a spectator, even in the broadest meaning of that term. I don't like to watch football games because I feel left out, unless one of the players is a friend with whom I can identify as he runs down the field with the ball.

For this reason, I decided to learn to use a movie camera for my Cape Horn adventure. I am trying to learn as much as I can about techniques that are, to me, quite new. I have already learned enough to know that, when I get back to shore, I will be interested in film editing, in methods of sound recording, and in all the other aspects of that art of which I have been so long in ignorance.

If, one day, I should discover that sailing has become nothing more than a mere repetition of techniques that I have learned, then I will certainly give up sailing. But, in my heart, I know that there will never come a day when the sea does not have something to teach me.

To put it in more concrete terms, let me take the example of Sir Francis Chichester. I hope to beat Chichester's record. Now, that is an honorable aim. At the same time, it must be said that my attempt is, above all, an act of homage to the man himself. It is Chichester who opened the road for those who come after him. He is the one who, by daring to confront the three capes, alone, on the clipper route, demonstrated that it was possible to do so. Since then, techniques have changed and equipment has been improved. My boat is larger and faster than his and is outfitted differently. All these things may mean that I will break his record; but they also mean that even if I succeed I will never equal his performance. What I want, by giving it my very best shot, is to be worthy of the example set by Sir Francis, to extend achievement in time, and thereby to engage in a race of my own against the shadow of the great clipper ships.

Things never stand still. It is part of human nature to go from one absorbing thing to the next, just as waves are in constant action and follow one another unceasingly. I have only one fear: that I will become bogged down or trapped in one job or one role.

Obviously, I have no intention of renouncing the ecstatic experience of being the first to cross a finish-line. That is a joy so intense and profound that it engulfs a man and leaves him weak and exhausted.

I had spent months, even years, before Newport, thinking and working for absolutely nothing except the moment that I would cross that line. When it happened, I was swept into seventh heaven—until the moment passed with surprising rapidity.

But, for a long time after Newport, I was at peace with myself. I was calm, relaxed. Happiness may well consist of establishing a rare harmony between what we are and what we do. But since we are constantly changing, we must also be ready always to look for another peak to scale, another task to undertake. For me, that peak, that task, has the craggy form of a somber, forbidding rock with a name that resounds like a sail luffing in the breeze: Cape Horn. It is no doubt an ambitious undertaking; a very high and difficult step for me to contemplate. But I have not the slightest doubt that, once I have taken that step, it will prove to be merely a step to something else. It does no good to reach a goal unless we leave something of ourselves along the way.

Monday, October 8.

There is a thin veil of clouds over the sky, but the moon is brilliantly reflected in the sea and Venus stands out, her splendor enhanced by a maidenly halo, through the veil. I feel now a familiar urge, a strong, inexpressible near-compulsion to be one with the air, the sky, the water, the wind, the sun, and the moon. I think my main reason for leaving Paris was that I saw so little of the sun there.

The morning meteorological report is good, and I've decided to set a course for Tristan da Cunha.

Today marks the five-thousandth mile at an average speed of seven knots. My previous record, set during the 3,000 miles of the Transatlantic, was six knots. I feel more certain than ever that I'll be able to beat the record set by Sir Francis Chichester and the clipper ships.

Tuesday, October 9.

I was awakened at 0600 hours by the compass alarm, informing me of a change in course. Set course at 130. I think that I've now pretty much passed through the Doldrums and I should soon encounter the southeast trade winds.

During the day, I heard that *Great Britain II* is only about twenty hours ahead of me. I'm delighted to know it—and surprised. To celebrate, I took a three-hour nap. Then, re-energized, I decided to hoist my large spinnaker, an enormous bubble of multicolored nylon, to take advantage of an aft wind.

Wednesday, October 10.

This morning, I awoke to find *Manureva* lying to, brought by the lee, and her bow northwest. Notwithstanding that setback, in the past twenty-four hours we covered 240 miles, for an average speed of 10 knots. We then crossed the Tropic of Capricorn, not with drums beating and trumpets blaring, but in a wall of fog and in a sea so rough that I was glued to the helm. At this speed, it's out of the question for me to think of leaving the helm. No automatic pilot yet invented can take the place of a human being there in rough seas. Only a man can pilot a boat according to the next wave or anticipate the movements of the boat. It's not easy for me. But on a journey like this one, and especially when I know that *Manureva* is moving at fifteen knots, a speed that no solitary sailor has achieved before, I am ready to make almost any sacrifice and to put up with any discomfort.

I've been brought by the lee twice already by the waves. Even so, it's still an enormous pleasure for me to pilot *Manureva* through such a sea. Imagine the thrill when the boat, already moving at considerable speed, is caught by a wave, lifted up, and then shot forward in an exhilarating burst of even greater speed.

Because I don't dare leave the helm, I've had to postpone until tomorrow my radio contact with R.T.L.

This evening there were great dark clouds in the sky, and the sun set with a splendid display of purples and golds. A bank of cumulo-nimbus is coming from the southeast, and it signals the arrival of a low pressure system. I've lowered the mizzen to reduce my speed, and I'm waiting for the squall. Still, my average speed is increasing, and this confirms me in my decision to alter my course to pass off Tristan da Cunha and then to hold *Manureva* on a straight course for the Cape of Good Hope.

Thursday, October 11.

The sky cleared completely at 0400 and the Southern Cross stretched out before me. The wind has risen, and I must try to take advantage of it. I ran up the mizzen, and we are moving at a good speed.

Once more, I took a three-hour nap. I suspect the time is coming when I won't be able to afford such luxuries.

I awoke to bad weather and vicious little squalls. I'll have to wait and see what the future holds as far as the weather is concerned. The weather maps from Buenos Aires are all good.

Friday, October 12.

Despite the trade-wind sky, the wind is from the west, a good sailing wind, and I now have every hope of being able to reach Sydney in the best time of the clippers. I'm keeping up, practically to the hour—in fact, to the minute and the second—with tall ships. Needless to say, morale is high aboard *Manureva!*

I've been using the spinnaker. I'm now also using my main staysail. That gives me about 1,300 square feet of sail up there. It's a very impressive sight, and I've tried to capture it on film.

Saturday, October 13.

Day follows day, but the days are not all alike. Today, the barometer is climbing and the wind is dropping. I've lowered my spinnaker and mizzen, and hoisted my genoa. Now, late in the afternoon, my 236 square feet of sail are hanging limp. There is not even enough of a breeze for the anemometer to work. I am on full automatic pilot.

The day ends in total, absolute calm. The sea is beautiful, with a westerly and southwesterly swell.

This is the end of my fifth week and it is time to figure out

61

my gains and losses. The use of that term seems somehow disrespectful. I've just heard it used on the radio on a broadcast about violence in the Mid-East.

Here are my figures: 1,339 miles between meridian points for the week, on a straight course. My average speed was almost eight knots.

Thus far, I've come a total of 5,934 nautical miles, for an average of 169.5 miles per day, with an average speed of seven knots.

The Whitbread Race goes on. Thursday, *Adventure* predicted that she would reach the Cape in two weeks. According to what I've heard from *Grand Louis,* the positions of the leading boats, in corrected time, are as follows: first, *Adventure;* second, *Kriter;* third, *Guia. Pen Duick VI* is now 400 miles off Rio with her new mast.

I got new information during my Saturday radio contact with R.T.L. In real time, it seems that *Great Britain II* is in the lead, and only *33 Export* is in a real position to challenge her. The other boats apparently have fallen victim to the calm weather to the north and the east.

In any case, the next few days will divide the boats up into the "Africans" and the "Brazilians," depending upon which continent they favor as they cross the South Atlantic. I expect that the first ones will arrive Sunday or Monday.

There has been no news from *Sayula* or from *Jakaranda.* Cape Town Radio has asked all ships to be on the lookout for them.

Sunday, October 14.

Since 0800, I've been using the large spinnaker on two booms. Earlier, I filmed the dawn from the port pontoon.

I received a weather map that promises good weather. Then

the sky clouded over, the barometer dropped several points, and the air has suddenly turned cool.

I've just seen my first albatross, a giant bird with a wingspan of no less than ten feet. It looked like a kind of cargo plane, with its large body and its absolutely unmoving wings.

The wind has now changed to the northeast and I made the necessary changes as quickly as I could, bringing down my 674-square-foot spinnaker and my 337-square-foot staysail, which I was using on the southerly course. I was just in time. The albatross was wheeling to port and, under his baleful stare, I did the same. I am now reaching an area of high winds and storms from the west. I'm using my jib and genoa.

If I had to give a fundamental rule for a solitary sailor enroute to Australia, it would be this: Go straight, straight, straight. Turn left at the first albatross, then relax and let the wind do the rest. It will carry you right along.

I talked to Jeff again this morning. We are still getting ready for the technical aspect of my layover in Sydney, and I asked him to make particularly certain that I would have the paint and varnish that I need for the hull. I might have to sand and refinish it, because I've had a problem with flaking. The varnish used at Lorient has turned out to be very unsatisfactory.

We ended our conversation on an optimistic note. I took the bull by the horns and announced that I would reach the Cape of Good Hope next Sunday. I think that I'm among the first three boats, behind *Great Britain* and *33 Export*.

Monday, October 15.

The wind is up and the sea is rough. I tried to do some filming but succeeded only in getting the camera thoroughly wet. Later, I did manage to get some footage of a magnificent sunset and a solitary dolphin sporting in the water.

I managed to get my friend Philippe Gildas on the radio, but there was so much interference that I couldn't get much help from him on various problems that I have as a neophyte cameraman—problems of speed, focus, filters for the zoom lens and telescopic sight, etc. My Beaulieu camera seems to be on the blink as the result of its bath this morning. Perhaps I'll be able to exchange it for another one, and deliver the film that I've already shot, if I can arrange a rendezvous at sea off the Cape of Good Hope.

Tuesday, October 16.

Between yesterday noon and today noon (my thirty-ninth day at sea), we covered 326 nautical miles, which sets a new record for a solitary sailor. I won't even try to explain how excited and delighted I am. Up to now, the 300-mile single time mark was an uncrossable barrier for sailors, except, of course, for the tall ships—the three- and four-masters of the last century—but even they had trouble in crossing it. At the moment, I'm in the middle of a deluge, a Niagara of seawater swirling over *Manureva*, but I'm in a kind of ecstasy and nothing seems to bother me.

According to my calculations, I'm five or six days off the Cape of Good Hope, and I feel like a winner. Despite the delays in the Bay of Biscay and the calms I've encountered, my time is almost exactly the same as that of *Cutty Sark* 100 years ago. I must say that I've been able to get excellent weather information, and thus have been able to choose my course carefully and take advantage of the weather. And for the past three days, I've been riding some particularly good isobars, with strong favorable winds.

All I have to do now is to keep shoveling the coal, so to speak. In effect, since I reached this area of good winds, *Manureva* is like a locomotive speeding down the track. All she needs is fuel, which, in this case, is wind instead of coal.

I must add, however, that at 0400, *Manureva* broached, and I had a devil of a time bringing her back. I was completely soaked—and the water was not exactly warm. But, since I had just computed my average speed during the four preceding hours at twelve knots, I took it all in stride.

It was a long morning, most of it taken up with difficult chores because of the seas and the wind. Nonetheless, at 0900, I had my regular daily contact with the boats in the race, at least with those that I can reach. *Adventure* and *Burton Cutter* are silent. *Grand Louis* and *33 Export* both tell me that that silence is deliberate; and the two latter boats are the only ones that can pick them up clearly.

The positions, on corrected time, seem to be: *Adventure, CS et RB, Kriter, Grand Louis, Guia, Burton Cutter,* and *33 Export.*

I used my radio contact with R.T.L. to sing a victory hymn to myself, announcing my position as 35° of southern latitude and enumerating the records that we've broken, telling how *Manureva* "literally cut through the waves and threw great torrents of water several yards into the air"—all in a delirium of joy.

Obviously, *Manureva* now requires my attention almost full-time, but I don't regret it. I've now covered 6,000 miles at an average speed of seven knots, compared to the 3,000 miles of the Transatlantic at an average speed of six knots. At the moment, my daily average is twelve knots!

During the evening I spoke to my family, once more gathered at Clamecy. I was able to tell them that during the night I would pass the Greenwich meridian (my longitude at present being 0.1°W). I also asked them to pass on *Kriter's* position to the Whitbread committee, which has been asking for it since morning.

Wednesday, October 17.

I talked with *Kriter* this morning. She has been becalmed for the past eighteen hours. I also contacted *33 Export,* dragging along at three knots, *Grand Louis,* and *Tauraga* which, under spinnaker and staysail, has covered 230 miles and says she is moving at between fifteen and eighteen knots.

Today's meridian confirms, with a comfortable margin, yesterday's figures (which, since the sky was cloudy, was only an estimate).

Toward noon, the sky cleared, and I settled down to check and recheck my computations to make sure that I had indeed covered 326 miles since picking up the wind. The actual figure I came up with was 312, on the basis of my log. But, on the basis of the current and other factors, several miles are added to that figure. The final figure for the period between October 15 and October 16, from meridian point to meridian point, is 320 miles measured in a straight line on the map. But the gain in longitude, if we are actually talking about twenty-three hours and thirty-nine minutes, is six nautical miles in twenty-four miles; i.e., 326 miles. (This figure would be confirmed later.)

I reached both Teura and my family this evening, but the contact was so poor that I could barely hear and I told them that I would try again the next day.

Conversations with my family are now more or less reduced to a lengthy monologue aimed at Jeff, who is taping the lists of things that have to be ordered for Sydney. Some of the things I will need have already been ordered—the paint, food, water. Here are just a few of those items, extracted from Jeff's transcribed lists:

Ask Albert for the material that I'm going to need for the lateral shrouds on the main mast, and have these made by S.A.R.M.A. in whatever diameter Albert says I should use.

Ask the Maritime Radio Company for the telegraphic manipulator that can be adapted to my equipment; and ask them for a manual, also.

Ask Victor to make another sea anchor for me, and order 200 feet of ¾ inch nylon line. (I've just reread Chichester and Moitessier, and I'm beginning to worry about Cape Horn!)

An assortment of ring and swivel-hook pulleys, most of which should be double.

Next year's nautical almanac (astronomical tables), which were not ready when I left.

Two spinnaker poles, two jib halyards, and halyards for the spinnaker, the mainsail, and mizzen.

Stainless-steel safety-hanks—the German ones I have are made of bronze and are too fragile.

Red deck paint, a winch handle, rivets, nuts and bolts.

A large roll of thick flannel for interior use (I've lost some in spots, but it's still effective as padding against bumps, and I'm having much less problem in this respect than I did in the past.)

The radio contact with my family, lists notwithstanding, were a source of comfort to me and were essential to my morale for the entire voyage as well as to my eventual success. If it had not been for my family, I wonder how much time I would have had to spend in Sydney, tracking down every last item on the interminable lists that I dictated to Jeff. How pleasant it is to be able to join that which is agreeable to that which is useful—in this instance, conversations with my family to the efficiency of my brother.

I also sent a telegram to *Tintin,* which was much less com-

67

plex than the lists because it was much less technical: "Fantastic ride and fantastic wind. A thousand miles in four days, and 326 miles yesterday in twenty-four hours. All records broken. Am between Tristan da Cunha and Good Hope on the route of the tall ships. Am within *Cutty Sark*'s time. Escorted by traditional albatrosses. Best, Alain Colas."

Thursday, October 18.

I talked to Teura at 0700 via Saint-Lys, for eight minutes. The contact was very good for four minutes. Everything is going well, and everything is falling into place for my arrival at Sydney.

At 0900, I had my usual contact with the racers and found out that *Burton Cutter* is 340 miles west-northwest of the Cape, while *33 Export* is still creeping along at two knots. According to yesterday's B.B.C. report, the corrected time positions are: *CS e RB, Adventure, Kriter, Guia.*

There is a cool wind from the west, and throughout the morning we moved along briskly in a dense fog. The water is rather rough, the result of crossing swells. Nonetheless, I'm using the large spinnaker and the main staysail. During the afternoon the fog dissipated, but I had the sun for only one hour before the clouds moved in and it began to drizzle.

Irritated and impatient, I'm engaged in a running battle— first, with the speed regulator, which is not sensitive enough to respond at less than seven or eight knots, and above all, with the Decca automatic pilot which keeps bearing to port. I can correct the deviation easily enough at the helm—but this means that I have to be at the helm constantly.

Everything has now changed: the low which seemed to be moving northeast has suddenly forked out toward the southeast and, if I had continued on the same course, I would have been becalmed. I must resign myself to going straight south. On the sea, as in life, I tend to be too optimistic, and all this happened just at the moment that I was about to catch up with *33 Export!*

Friday, October 19.

This was not a very good day. It began in fog and drizzle with occasional squalls. The sky was cloudy and the water became increasingly rough. Moreover, it is cold and the temperature in the cabin did not climb above 57°F. I do not feel quite up to par, despite a beef bourguignon, lovingly simmered, which I prepared in order to buck myself up. In spite of the vitamins that I'm taking, I seem to be running at something less than full power.

With the weather the way it is, I cannot take my bearings, but I estimate my position as 37°18'S and 07°24'E. My navigation reflects my general mood and is somewhat hesitant. *Manureva* was brought by the lee before I could bring myself to haul down the mizzen and then the spinnaker and send up first the light genoa and then the heavy one. Then the wind fell to zero, putting an end to a perfect day.

Saturday, October 20.

The bad weather is pursuing us, and I am confined below with my radio and my black thoughts.

Outside, the porpoises and the albatrosses continue to be the only sentient beings that I have seen for a month. Where would I be without my radio contacts? Even those today are confined to news of the race.

69

To cap it all, the Cape Town Radio forecasts are pessimistic. As though to confirm those gloomy predictions, the colors of the sunset promise an impending battle with the elements. In fact, I'm already having a devil of a time keeping *Manureva* on course.

Another splendid day. I console myself as much as I can with the tally for the week: 1,472 miles, for an average of 210 miles per day. The total distance covered is now 7,406 miles in forty-two days. Daily average: 176 miles. Average speed: 7.3 knots. Exciting figures.

Saturday, October 21.

The sea is very rough and the crossing swells have kept me jumping all morning. I have not even been able to take my usual radio break at 0900. I wonder what is happening to the boats.

Later in the day, I learned that *Burton Cutter* took the lead last night. What a dark horse that boat has been. *Adventure,* trailing by 100 miles, is expected today.

Although today is Sunday, it will hardly be a day of rest. There are several broken slides atop the mainsail and I've had to haul it down. I hoisted my jib and began a battle against the sea that lasted, by the clock, for three hours. I had to shinny up about a third of the mast to unblock the slides with a hammer and cold chisel—an exercise that I am not eager to repeat.

All this work simply to reach the Cape of Good Hope! Discouraged, I decided to have lunch early, at 1130, and went below leaving the sails exactly as they were. The sea is still rough, and the waves are from thirteen to seventeen feet high. I think that a single long radio session with *Grand Louis* would do me a lot of good right now.

There was a real sunset this evening, and shortly thereafter I could see stars in the sky! Nonetheless, I am going to wait to see what happens.

Monday, October 22.

I was right not to trust the stars last night. The sea is very rough and I'm being thrown about like a cork by twenty- or twenty-five-foot waves.

Last night, not without a touch of irony, France-Inter announced my position as "off the Cape of Good Hope, having covered 306 miles in the past twenty-four hours." There seems to have been a breakdown in communications somewhere along the line.

The sky was ominously cloudy all day and squall followed squall. The Cape Town weather bureau broadcast a "wind warning" in the area toward which we are, with such difficulty, trying to head.

I am cold and tired. Fortunately, late in the evening, I was able to contact R.T.L. and my family in Clamecy. I gave my report for the sixth week at sea, my general average, an account of the wind these past few days, my acrobatics on the mast, and so forth. From my family I received the psychological and technical support that I needed. What foolishness it was for me to head east and then to end up following the depression for four days in a row. Now I have to set a course for the Cape in a really heavy sea. I have been searching for a ray of hope in the distant lightning; but even the night brings no comfort or relief. The spectacle at least is worth watching.

Some of the boats in the race have been able to reach the Cape and therefore to get some well-earned rest from the weather. *Burton Cutter* arrived Saturday night, followed by *Adventure* on Sunday afternoon. (*Adventure* is in the lead on corrected time.) *Great Britain* reached port Sunday night.

Tuesday, October 23.

I missed my regular 0900 radio break this morning because I had to repair a break in the cable of the anemometer. Topside, tossed about by the swells, I glimpsed a cargo ship on the horizon, heading east. It is the first one that I've seen in a long time.

I heard, while I was doing some needlework in the cabin, that *33 Export* has entered Table Bay and is only five or six miles away from her destination. The last time I spoke to *33 Export*, her crew wished me a good wind and Godspeed!

Wednesday, October 24.

Oh, what irony! The wind has died down completely, and I was becalmed all night.

At 0900, I heard that *33 Export* did indeed reach Cape Town last night (she is tenth in corrected time) and that *Grand Louis*, after being becalmed for six hours during the afternoon, is now moving at ten knots despite a torn spinnaker and a defective helm, thanks to an inside wheel.

It is a very long day and I am spending most of it in my continuing battle with the sea. It took me two hours to haul down the mizzen, because the slides are defective. In the past seven days, I've covered less distance than in the preceding three days. And, despite my lack of speed, I am not getting a moment of rest. I cannot even eat in peace. My spaghetti dinner was interrupted twice by *Manureva* broaching.

I dictated a telegram to *Tintin,* via Saint-Lys Radio, to sum up my week: "Three days in a wind storm and rough seas with waves twenty to twenty-five feet high in order to get around Cape of Good Hope. Difficult climb up mainmast to disengage mainsail. Sewed after dark holding flashlight in my mouth and under my arm. How I'd love to spend one night at

Cape to repair boat and captain! Now heading for Australia. Cordially, Alain Colas.''

During my contact with R.T.L., I developed the same highlights, explaining in detail my problems with the slides and the blocking of the Decca automatic pilot—but also describing the phosphorescence of the waves.

Near 1900 on Wednesday, October 24, my forty-seventh day at sea, I crossed the longitude of the Cape of Good Hope. Hurrah, I say feebly. One stage of the journey is over (and without putting into port). All in all, it did not present any really serious problems.

In my mind, I go over the broad lines from the beginning till now, with a certain amount of satisfaction in a job well done.

Now, off the Cape of Good Hope, at the crossroads of two oceans, I feel like celebrating! Except that, just as I was about to cross the longitude of the Cape, the sea started up again and I began a rather frightening dash over the waves at more than twenty knots. For a while when the wind was down, I realized that drifting was dangerous in those waves, and that speed was absolutely necessary. At this point, I must take into account that ordinary everyday navigation is no longer enough, and the time has come for some pretty fancy sailing. This is a serious game, and I must learn the rules as fast as I can.

The first rule, no doubt, is that of prudence. I have lowered the mainsail and the number one jib and hoisted my number two jib, which gives me a cruising speed of eight knots.

After all, every mile covered until now was pretty much the work of *Manureva*. Absorbed in steering and maintenance chores, I did not have time to be bored. And, if the thousand little shipboard jobs I had to do every day left me little time for rest, it was all to allow me finally to see the spectacle of the elements unleashed before my eyes.

Perhaps a rundown of my daily routine aboard *Manureva* will give some idea of what I mean.

Rise with the dawn for a look at the sky, which results in the first moment of joy or of disgust. (The night was spent, in either case, broken into sections: two or three hours of sleep at a time, interspersed with periods at the helm. Sleep was reduced further when we were near shore or when there were freighters in the area.) Then, scan the horizon, and make minor adjustments, before extinguishing the running lights.

After a quick breakfast, the first session with the sextant—before my radio break. Then, position finding. Next is the time for urgent chores, such as repairing torn sails and so forth; or, if there are none, for writing in my schoolboy copybooks: red cover for my log, yellow for radio contacts.

At the end of the morning, weather permitting, it is time to observe the meridian: high noon, which, with a few mental calculations, gives me my exact latitude. Immediately thereafter, enter the latitude on the chart and compute *Manureva*'s position. Finally, draw the course to be followed.

The first real break comes with lunch, followed by coffee. Then I hook up my generator to make my various radio contacts and, afterward, to recharge the batteries.

The afternoon begins with work at the helm and, if circumstances allow, either reading or—the wind permitting—meditation over the charts. This is my time for thinking, for nostalgia, and for hoping. I alternate visits to the helm, short naps or cups of tea, another session with the sextant just to check my earlier calculations, and the afternoon is at an end. At dusk, when the stars begin to come out, a further check with the H.O. 249 tables will remove any lingering doubt.

It is then time to begin preparation of the evening meal. Hot food does wonders for morale. Moreover, as a good Frenchman, I have always been careful to honor the traditions of my country in the care that I take in preparing my food.

No doubt, the Indian Ocean will upset my daily routine somewhat. But then, that is its right, and I will not argue.

74

4

A sea of troubles

Thursday, October 25.

At 0500 the sea was already rough and I came topside to find *Manureva* brought by the lee. But the beauty of the morning light on the waves, and the albatrosses wheeling overhead with their wings gilded by the rising sun, made me forget about the problems of navigation. I stood transfixed.

Finally, I shook myself awake and hoisted the light jib.

Trouble came with the afternoon. After I raised the starboard genniker and hauled down the jib, the genniker halyard snapped and I had to fish the sail out of the freezing water. I then ran up the port genniker—to discover that the rollers were not working properly. The whole thing is going to have to be reworked.

Meanwhile, as I was working, the wind shifted to the southeast. I decided to leave everything as it was and go below to change. I had had enough, for the moment.

After dinner, I tried again. Nothing seemed to be working properly. I prepared the jib, hauled down the genniker. The halyard was jammed atop the mast. With a great deal of trouble I managed to hoist the mainsail. Then I noticed that the top of the casing on the speed-regulator was loose. I did everything that I could to straighten things out before trying to get some sleep. By then it was midnight, and I was so exhausted that I could barely drag myself to my berth.

The only good moment of the day was when *33 Export,* in port, reached me by radio. She is third on handicap. *Kriter* reached port last night.

I almost forgot to mention the fabulous sunrise this morning!

Friday, October 26.

I was awakened several times by the alarm that signals a change in course. I got up and disengaged *Manureva* from the course to which she had been turned by a strong swell from the south-southwest.

My problems continue with a vengeance. I had to remove the mizzen slides and substitute those of the storm trysail, and then change four battens before sending up the mizzen. Next, I had to try to unblock the automatic pilot—straddling the support just above the wake and pounding away with a hammer and a center punch. Before it was over, I had a nasty cut on my hand.

I've decided that I deserve some sort of consolation, and I am going to prepare myself a gargantuan meal—even before taking care of my hand.

My decision seems to have mollified the sea gods. The water is not nearly as rough as it was. I've run up the jib, and we've begun to look like a boat again. Finally, the wind has picked up.

Blessings always arrive in pairs. I've been able to contact

Cape Town Radio. They've given me their listening frequencies and we've decided on a working frequency.

Things seem to be going better.

Tonight, there's a celebration aboard *33 Export*.

Saturday, October 27.

Happiness is clean pajamas and dry sheets. Unhappiness is having them and not appreciating them.

Once more, at 0500, I found *Manureva's* bow turned north. The alarm did not ring and it is obviously not working. But the sun is shining! What a pleasure, after the endless days of gray sky. I'm taking advantage of it to dry out my bread on deck.

Around noon, *Manureva* suddenly broached and I had to bring down the staysail. Even when things appear to be going well, it seems that the elements are in league against me.

At sunset, a picture postcard spectacle reconciled me to life: the sun, at sea level, suddenly touched the waves and transformed the sea into a mass of molten gold stretching to the horizon as far as I could see. After such a display, what right have I to complain about anything?

The tally of my seventh week at sea: 890 nautical miles. Obviously, I'm losing ground. My record for the past week looks like that of the first week, and it's far below that of the preceding week during which we covered 1,472 miles. Even so, I've done a total of 8,096 miles in seven weeks. for an average daily distance of 165 miles. I've lost only one-third of a knot from the average speed.

I have a bit of a technical problem. For the first time, my dead reckoning position and my computed position are at variance. I must admit that, for the past week, I've been doing my calculations by the seat of my pants, since there was no sun. And this morning's calculation is suspect because of our little "accident" right in the middle of it. I'm going to have to find out what's wrong.

Sunday, October 28.

All night long, lying in my berth, I could feel *Manureva* tossing in the waves and I could hear the grinding of the sheets. These were not reassuring sounds. I went topside and untangled the jib sheet from the boom.

We broached again at dawn this morning, as the result of squalls and a southwest wind. A more serious accident: several mainsail battens are broken. I tried to haul down the mainsail, but, of course, the slides were sticking. I ended up with the same solution as before: climbing up the mast and doing another trapeze number in a rough sea.

There was not enough time this afternoon for me to change all the slides and replace the four broken upper battens, even though I did not even take time for lunch. I grabbed a handful of raisins and a dextrose tablet on the run.

At 2000, I got the weather report from Cape Town very clearly. Then I called Clamecy. Jeff was not there, but I launched into all sorts of technical explanations which my father seemed to understand. In any event, he was taping the conversation, and no doubt Jeff will be able to do whatever is necessary. I gave my position, estimated as of this evening, as 40°S and 30°E, explaining that I had probably lost at least three days because of various problems. Then I explained, at length and in great detail, what those problems were: first, the automatic pilot that blocks to the left (a problem that only C.R.M. can solve); and especially my troubles with the rust-proof slides that Albert made for me. I asked for a system, to be installed on the booms of the mainsail and the mizzen, for adjusting the sail shape. I gave Victor Tonnerre the go-ahead to make me a tall boy staysail and a small running spinnaker. I am also going to need new foul weather gear, since I tore mine to shreds during my trapeze act atop the mast. I would like Equinoxe to design oilskins for me that have a safety harness built into the jacket; there are times when I can't use the conventional harness because I get tangled up in it. At this point in the conversation, I had to pause to reassure Papa, who was quite upset, that I always tie a line around my body—which, in fact, I do when the sea gets really rough. I also asked for a book on birds so that I can get to know those that I see and will see around the boat. I added to the already long list of spare parts I would need. And, finally, I once more began my technical explanations about the slides to make sure that there would be no misunderstanding of the problem.

I could sense that Papa was worried and I tried to reassure him. I told him about the problems that I was having with my generator and transmitter so that he would not be concerned if, in the days ahead, I was not able to contact the family. I ended by promising that I would take time to rest, and to allow *Manureva* to rest, and that I would continue at reduced speed for a few days longer—despite the wind and despite the problems of the last week that had already delayed me. I still hoped to reach Sydney in a total of eighty days. My closing words were designed to put his mind at ease: "There aren't any more problems," I said. "Everything is under control. I'm very optimistic, and I promise not to take any chances with the boat."

The whole conversation with my father lasted twenty-nine minutes. I have no doubt that I dragged it out because I needed the boost in morale that contact with my family gives me. In reassuring Papa, I was actually reassuring myself. It always helps to have someone worrying about you.

Monday, October 29.

It's starting again. At one in the morning, I was awakened by the alarm. *Manureva* was changing course. The wind was up and we had to veer about—and then veer about again.

It seems to me that the great west winds in these parts, which I've heard so much about, are really a series of depressions with a permanent rotation and a corresponding variation in intensity. I think that the best solution is to navigate normally; that is, to sail according to the weather and to avoid either panicking in a very strong blow or becoming too enthusiastic in a stable west wind.

The latest news I have of the race (in the last few days, I've given up my 0900 radio break in favor of an afternoon session at 1500) is as follows: *Grand Louis* reached the Cape on October 26, and *Tauraga* on October 27. *33 Export* is already in dry dock for repairs. I don't expect I will see any of the boats again until the next stage: the route to Cape Horn. The boats are scheduled to leave on the Cape Town–Sydney leg of the race on November 7, at least according to France-Inter. Regulations require departure between the seventh and twelfth day after the arrival of 70% of the participants.

Tuesday, October 30.

We had gusts of wind during the night of forty to fifty knots, as a front of squalls accompanied by lightning passed by. With the boat pitching and tossing, I hauled down the mainsail to avoid taking any chances. The barometer was falling, and I stayed awake to wait for the blow.

Then the sea gradually calmed down, the wind shifted to the west, and the sky was perfectly clear by the end of the morning. The barometer had climbed again. I cannot make any sense out of this.

I ran up the genoa to take advantage of the waves. My somewhat timid precautions during the night probably cost me about forty miles. With waves like these, there's no doubt that the helmsman makes all the difference. There is no Decca electric pilot, and no Gianoli speed-regulator, that can prevent a boat from broaching at the end of a slide. The only thing to do is to reduce your sail in order to control your spurts of speed.

The sky is covered with stars, and I celebrated by having boiled potatoes and butter in approximately equal amounts. I had hardly swallowed the last mouthful when the wind shifted again to the northwest and the swell brought us by the lee. I tried to get out of it as well as I could. But, two hours later with the waves like something out of a nightmare and gusts of forty to fifty knots, I decided to take no chances. I would lower the mainsail and use the running jib. If I expected trouble with the mainsail, I was not mistaken. It came tumbling down and, before I knew what was happening, the battens landed on my nose. If that was not bad enough, one can imagine what is involved in furling a mainsail in a fifty-knot gale. It will be a long time before I forget that particular experience.

Wednesday, October 31.

Squalls and waves kept me on watch all night to try to avoid being brought by the lee. I was successful until about 0500; and then, in trying to correct, I broke five of the mizzen battens.

These waves, with all the luffing and sudden heeling, make me break out in a cold sweat. I don't know what the solution is. How can one sail in this kind of sea and these variable winds? Perhaps the most I can hope for is to make some small headway on a southern route by hauling down the mainsail and keeping the mizzen and jib. By 2200, I could barely lift my arms and I had to give it up in order to get at least a few hours of sleep.

When I awoke, the sea was not as rough and things were going better. The barometer was rising, and I was even able to have breakfast while listening to France-Inter.

I spent the entire afternoon working on the mizzen, replacing broken battens and defective slides, while a magnificently red sunset gave a touch of Hollywood to the operation. There was no one to see me working in full color—fortunately, because, at the last moment, a sudden gust resulted in three more broken battens in the mainsail.

Thursday, November 1.

Finally, a peaceful night, I snuggled under the covers and got some sleep, with a hot-water bottle for company. There is an Arctic—or rather, Antarctic—chill in the air. Later in the afternoon, I closed the hatch and lit the heater until the cabin was warm.

The sea is still rough and the waves massive enough to get us up to speeds too high to register on the speedometer. The only thing I can do is to use the running jib, take in reefs in the main and mizzen, and then luff.

Friday, November 2.

A slight increase in speed woke me and made me sit bolt upright in my berth. There had been nothing on the barometer to indicate any change in the weather. I made my way to the bubble of the interior wheel just when a brutal gust of over fifty knots shook the boat and then carried it along. Barefooted and in my pajamas, I paid out the sheets and hauled down what I could of the sails. By then, my pajamas were in shreds and I was soaked and chilled to the bone. Even so, I had the feeling that I had just had a narrow escape. *Manureva* was now moving at a speed that I had never before experienced—perhaps as much as thirty knots—and starboard of the central hull I could see nothing but water. The mainsail was jammed at mid-mast. I had been able to haul down only the running jib and the mizzen. Fortunately, I had taken in two reefs everywhere to reduce my sail—a precautionary measure that, last night when I went to bed, I assured myself was making much ado about nothing.

In the cabin, I turned on the heater and rubbed myself down with eau de cologne. I was trembling with cold, and perhaps, retroactively, with fear. Once in dry clothes and reasonably warm under the bubble where the heat tends to gather, I put on my oilskins and lowered the mainsail with the winch. There was considerable damage: four of the upper slides were broken as well as five battens, two eyelet holes.

Once the wind slackened somewhat, I made slow headway under my running jib and reefed mizzen, while giving my full attention to handling the boat. Finally, I decided to go back to bed (thanking my lucky stars that I had awakened when I did) and somehow managed to sink into peaceful and refreshing slumber.

The sea was calmer during the day, and the sky gradually began to clear from the west. We even had a trade-wind sunset. What, I wonder, is in store for us next?

In the evening, I rinsed out my pajamas and underwear in fresh water, no doubt wasting some of my precious store. But it makes up in morale what it loses in water.

I was able to raise Saint-Lys today for a contact with R.T.L. and, later, with my parents. I've been trying to do this for four days, without success on any frequency that I tried.

I've been in the Indian Ocean now for about thirty-six hours, and thus far I've had nothing but one blow after another. I spend my time maneuvering, and repairing damages because my sails are constantly being abused.

Sometimes, when *Manureva* was lying to, twenty-five-foot waves would come along and "shoot" us forward like an empty can in a gutter. Then, as soon as I repaired the damage from the previous night, a new squall would arise and I would have to start all over again. The winds shifted constantly from northwest to southwest, passing by the east; and then began another similar round. There would have been the devil to pay if *Manureva* had not been able somehow to maneuver accordingly.

Despite all these problems, my average speed remains at ten knots, which does a great deal to keep my morale from slipping. I must confess, nonetheless, that I am very eager to leave these difficult latitudes and get to Sydney. I must be careful, however. Since the incident of the other night, when *Manureva* took off like a speedboat, I have been very cautious. The least little waver in the barometer, the slightest threatening hue in the sky, and I reduce sail.

Saturday, November 3.

Last night, I happened to get up for no particular reason other than to see if everything was all right and if the boat was handling the waves properly. It was pure luck that I happened to be on deck when we were struck by sudden gusts of forty or fifty knots. There was no warning at all. The sky was a mass of stars, and there were none of the clouds that normally presage squalls. The barometer had not budged. And yet, there I was: in an incredible wind, trying to lower the sails. I didn't even have time to put on my boots or my oilskins, and just barely enough time for the safety harness. The whole thing had a nightmare quality about it as, my hands and feet bleeding, I struggled first to haul down the 360 square feet of spinnaker, and then to hold it down in the wind, before sending up the running jib.

It seemed that it would take hours just to warm up again, and I was exhausted.

I estimate my position to be 40°30'S and 55°30'E, but I do not know for certain.

In making my tally for the past week I was pleasantly surprised. In spite of all the problems I've had, I've covered almost 1,500 miles, which makes a daily average of over 200 miles. That is a new solo record for me; but it is a record that I'm paying a high price for, and that does not please me as much as it should. I could almost say that it leaves me cold.

I have to remind myself that the whole purpose of this voyage is to rival the records set by the clipper ships. The Indian Ocean's welcome, however, has been so lacking in warmth, and I've had to spend so much time maneuvering and making repairs, that I find it hard to be terribly enthusiastic.

Certainly, I didn't expect the Indian Ocean to be easy sailing. I was well aware that these high latitudes, the "roaring forties," are very difficult. Still, I didn't expect things to be quite so difficult or to last so long. This is really a sea of troubles, where the waves toss boats around and the winds blow without relief and without mercy.

My consolation: we've covered 9,579 miles, and it is only another 1,000 miles to Amsterdam Island. After that, 3,000 miles to Bass Strait, then 500 to Sydney. A total of 4,500 miles. I've already come two-thirds of the way.

Still, I'm exhausted, and I've decided to change latitudes. I may lose time, but it will be worth it.

At 1300 GMT I had an excellent connection with R.T.L.

My mood was so somber that I think I must have worried them.

I spent the day hoisting first the storm spinnaker and then the mizzen.

The sea is rough and, at times, the waves are twenty feet high. There's nothing more tiring than trying to navigate when a good sailing wind alternates suddenly with violent gusts, in a cycle that follows only its own unpredictable logic.

The last rays of the sun today transformed the sky and ocean into a cathedral of golden light. I felt an urge to pray.

Sunday, November 4.

Around midnight, a few sudden spurts of speed made me haul down the sails as a precautionary measure.

Thanks to a decent meridian, I've been able to pinpoint my position at 39°9′S and 60°50′E. My earlier estimates were, as I suspected, wrong.

I spent the afternoon steering, but not always effectively. After being brought by the lee, in one instance, I hauled down the staysail in order to use the storm spinnaker. I was then going to send up the staysail again. But then I noticed that the top of the mizzenmast was bent over like a fishing pole. Immediately, I decided to haul down everything as fast as I could. It is not easy to find the right sail for this place.

I also had to repair the mainsail (still the battens and the slides) and to tinker with the relays of the Decca pilot according to the instructions I had received from the C.R.M. Further experiments with the sails will have to wait until tomorrow. I've become very cautious as far as night sailing is concerned. At midnight, for example, the barometer was as steady as it could be; but I had seen a red sunset and that had bothered me.

Monday, November 5.

The swell became less violent during the night, but we still were brought by the lee twice because of the waves.

At dawn, the sky reminded me of Carl Dreyer's film, *Ordet:* a covering of dense clouds transfixed by columns of golden light falling into a sea that is a study in motion.

I've hooked up the Decca, but its sole reaction now is to push the helm hard to starboard—with results that can be imagined. I will have to get hold of C.R.M. again.

I am trying a zigzag course now, luffing off to leeward and then sailing by the lee before moving forward again after a few minutes of very slow progress. What is the solution? Should I remain at the tiller all the time, or try to work out something with the gennikers so that they can be overridden by the tiller? Whatever it is, it will have to be something for use exclusively in the Pacific.

I heard on France-Inter that *Pen Duick VI* arrived in Rio today and will leave Wednesday.

Tuesday, November 6.

I was in and out of bed all night because of the waves and heeling and jibing.

I contacted Cape Town and then R.T.L., but I had to break contact in the middle in order to haul down the mainsail. There were gusts of fifty knots, and the waves were unbelievable. I was using only a running jib and even that was too much. The barometer is falling. I think that I am about 300 miles west-southwest of Saint Paul and Amsterdam Islands.

It is 55°F in the cabin—cold enough for me to turn on the heat. But I must conserve fuel since I need it for things other than heat. Radio contact, for example. Besides, when it's cold

87

in the cabin, it's easier for me to make the transition from inside to outside when I go on deck to struggle with the sails. Also, to help save my batteries, I asked R.T.L. today to pass on its information to *Tintin*. I thought of sending the magazine a telegram via Cape Town, but it would have taken forever. Since the telegram would have been in French, I would have had to spell every single word.

The sea is becoming really dangerous. I am using my number two jib now, but *Manureva* occasionally heels so that my hair stands on end. Some of the gusts of wind are incredible. I've had to close off the ventilators with wooden panels and seal off the hatch. It is now a matter of survival.

The wind is howling through the rigging with the same sound that used to keep me awake at night when the winter wind howled through the cedar trees at my parents' house.

Wednesday, November 7.

We were tossed about like a cork all night, and I didn't dare close my eyes for a moment.

In the morning, the fog was so thick that it seemed daylight would never come. It is drizzling now and the sea is in utter confusion, with strong swells from both the west and the north. The waves are sometimes seven or eight meters high.

In spite of everything, I must put on some sail and continue. I've decided to use the light foresail and simply let ourselves be carried by the wind. Then, during the afternoon, I ran up the mizzen. The barometer is still falling, and the weather is more and more ominous.

As night was falling and I was trying to reef the mizzen, *Manureva* suddenly heeled so heavily that I had to hold on for dear life. In a panic, I brought down the mizzen; and I was cured once and for all of the desire for more than an absolute minimum of sail in this weather. I went below, shivering, my legs trembling like reeds.

The relative proximity of Saint Paul and Amsterdam worries me and I am trying to head in a southerly direction. As chance would have it, today is the day that we have fog—just when I particularly need visibility to relieve my anxiety about reefs and rocks.

I've had no radio contact today. I miss my friends on the Whitbread boats, who were such good company.

I've been at sea for two months now. I will not be sorry when it's over.

Thursday, November 8.

My silent prayers have been answered. The sea is still rough, but the sky is clearing and, as a sign of victory, I ran up the mizzen.

I am now in the second half of my trek across the Indian Ocean as the sky continues to clear. The barometer is climbing and so is my morale. As I cross the longitude of Saint Paul and Amsterdam Islands, my mood is definitely "up."

The improved weather notwithstanding, the repairs go on. I spent the afternoon fixing the battens and slides of the mainsail, the mizzen battens, and so forth. Naturally, I cut my hand to ribbons, first on the handle of the winch and then by getting it caught under the mainsail boom. Even so, a cup of hot tea takes precedence over first aid.

I feel that I'm getting too close to the Antarctic ice. I've never seen the Southern Cross so high in the sky. My estimated position is 43°16′S.

Manureva continues to behave well; but, just to set my mind completely at rest, I will haul down the genoa tonight and hoist the running jib.

Friday, November 9.

Today the weather is not nearly so promising: fog and driz-zle. The Decca so-called automatic pilot is still not working properly, and I am obliged to make up for its inadequacies myself. In the general grayness of the day, and since I am unable to raise Perth on the radio, there is nothing for me to do but wait. I am not unduly concerned. The barometer is steady; but lately the barometer has not been the most dependable guide to the weather.

In the evening, the wind shifted to the southeast and I ran up the genoa again. At 2000, I had excellent radio contact with R.T.L. directly through Saint-Lys Radio. I had been trying to reach R.T.L. for two days through Australia. I then spoke with Jeff. I took advantage of both occasions to go over the past week, telling my correspondents about the tension and worry of the liquid hell that was my lot for several days. It is not easy for a sailor to confess such things; but I must admit that there were times during that week when I was afraid. The strong west winds that I encountered just past the Cape of Good Hope gave me an insight into these high latitudes about which so little is known, where the power of the sea and the wind surpasses anything in my previous experience.

After an incredible sunset the sea seemed to awake and stir. I've already experienced winds of all kinds, lasting from twenty-four hours to thirty-six hours. At most, they went on for two days. And here, the least stiffening of the breeze raises up liquid mountains that necessitate a constant struggle. And that was not all. Toward the middle of the Indian Ocean, a sudden northwest wind arose. There was already a strong swell with waves from twenty to twenty-seven feet high. Now, with the northwest wind, the sea became absolutely apocalyptic—the kind of sea that one does not see even in movies, but that a sailor sees in his mind's eye when he imagines what awaits him at Cape Horn. To picture it, imagine walls of water moving toward each other with incredible force, then meeting in indescribable chaos at a precise point.

Manureva, of course, was thrown about, groaning in agony. One would have to hear this festival of sound to appreciate it: the howling of the wind, rising as if from the depths of the sea, becoming louder and louder, and then falling silent for a moment before beginning again on another progressively louder pitch; the crashing of the waves around the boat; the shock of the water as it smashes against the hull and leaps toward the sky in an explosion of spray and foam; *Manureva,* shrieking in anguish until it seems that she must succumb; the moaning of the rigging.

When I saw those pyramidal waves, I could not bring myself either to watch their movement or to estimate their volume. But I knew that the weight of each molecule of water, combined with that of its neighbors, was rushing upon us. Then, at the very moment that I expected the wave to break over us, it seemed to pause for a fraction of an instant, as though it were deliberately pausing to make sure that its aim was correct, and that *Manureva* was indeed directly in its path. Usually, *Manureva* was spared the breaking of the wave—as though that momentary hesitation had given her enough time to remove herself from its path. But it happened occasionally that she did not escape; and then the masts shook continually, the shrouds moaned, and the sea seemed to bury everything. There was water everywhere and the drains in the deck of the bridge were not large enough to allow all the water to escape.

During this scene from the Inferno, I was in the cabin. I had already done all that I could above. It was now up to *Manureva* to show what she was made of. There were moments, I admit, when I had my doubts; times when it seemed inevitable that she would be thrown stern over stem by the very force of the water. Yet, there was nothing I could do but wait in the cabin, where I had already blocked every opening with hastily cut pieces of wood pounded into place with a hammer. And there were moments when an appeal for protection from above rose spontaneously within me.

The cabin itself was as fitted for survival as I could make it, with its food and water supply, its radio buoys, and its emergency exit in the bottom of the boat. I had made it as secure and watertight as possible, so that if anything happened, I could hold out there as long as possible. I was locked in as though I were in a safe to which only I had the combination—since, obviously, there was no one else around to open it. Which is not to say that I was by any means comfortable. I was cold; and with every wave I was hurled about and tossed from side to side. But, more than anything else, my discomfort was due to that sense of dread which, from time to time, turned my stomach to ice. To my credit, however, I must say that though I felt fear, I was never paralyzed by it. My mind was always alert and I was aware of what would have to be done if worse came to worse. It was the kind of fear that makes one active rather than passive in the face of danger.

As soon as I could, I called Clamecy and told my brother that I would maintain my position at between 40°S and 43°S. I repeated these figures several times, with emphasis, but without going into too much detail; I did not want to upset my parents. I hoped that Jeff, who had done some sailing with me, would understand what I was saying and be aware of what was happening. It should be obvious how much confidence I had that *Manureva* and I would survive the night!

Eventually, the sea calmed. Now, I am under way without too much trouble from the still monstrous waves hurrying in *Manureva*'s wake. But I am still in the middle of this gray, depressing stretch of ocean, this veritable sea of troubles, without any sign of life around me except for the birds. Despite moments of great beauty—for the ocean's power has a kind of beauty, as does the intensity of the stars at night—this is a place of despair in which a man should not linger; a place of sadness in which an intruder must have a stout heart.

Navigating in these waters presents special problems. I am referring not only to those frequent occasions when the waves are so high they resemble moving mountains and the sixty-seven and a half foot *Manureva* is tossed about like a trihulled straw, or when the wind is strong enough to lift a boat right out of the water. Even in calm—which is to say, in abnormal—weather, it is difficult to handle a boat in these icy waters. I never understood before the term "roaring forties." It no doubt refers to the winds, which sound like wild animals roaring in triumph just as they bring down their prey.

After rounding the Cape of Good Hope, after the excellent conditions encountered in the South Atlantic, it did not take me long to realize that I was using too much sail for the Indian Ocean's sudden gusts of wind, and that this was causing my halyards to break. I also realized that, even after these gusts, the sea remained rough for a long time. A boat cannot heave to indefinitely, even though there are times when she must simply allow herself to be carried along by the waves. In such instances, the solution is to hoist one's sails as quickly as possible; because the best way to get away is to go forward. The art of sailing is largely a matter of foresight, of weighing all the factors involved, almost to the point of counting the clouds in the sky. There is a risk involved in "opening up" the boat and heeling at the angle that she takes on the vertical wall of the waves; and there is also a risk in losing control after a strong gust of wind. A sailor has to be able to sense the dangers and the perils in every situation and make the right decision when, for example, faced with a more or less violent and unexpected squall. He must be able to choose between the risks of reducing his sail and those of going even faster.

Most often, even in very strong wind, I prefer to keep sail up—although this may mean hours of tension and the necessity for keeping constant watch to see what is happening. If the sea becomes too rough, then it is time to consider giving in and hauling down sail. But I consider that only as a last resort.

In a strong northwest wind, there is always the danger of being carried far south of my route. Sometimes we sail along the edge of the Antarctic ice; and, since I want to sleep peacefully at night, I have absolutely no desire to venture into iceberg territory.

Despite all these complications, I have gradually fallen into a routine. When the wind picks up, I take in sail. When it dies down a bit, we start up again. Squalls or sudden gusts mean that I must prepare for battle. The only trouble is that all these maneuvers, and the repairs that they always entail, leave me no free time. In the Atlantic, I had time to read. Now, I have no free time at all. In fact, my leisure time has been reduced to the few moments that I can snatch for a cup of hot coffee or tea. It is a kind of animal life in which, at odd times of the day and night, I simply crumple into a corner and sleep like a rock, usually still wearing my boots and oilskins. It goes on in an unbroken cycle: steer, steer, sleep; steer, sleep, and so on. I am going to have to do something about it and make up my mind to read a chapter a day, or even a few pages, just to regain my equilibrium.

My time is devoured by the endless stress of repairs that I must make every day. Sudden squalls mean that I have to haul down the sails like a madman; and this, in turn, means that sails are torn and battens are broken, which will take me hours to sew and repair. These strong winds are making kindling of the battens. The slides, which hold a sail to the mast and allow it to be raised and lowered, have suffered enormous damage and some of their parts are jammed in the aluminum

94

of the mast. Then, of course, there are the broken halyards. When they break, they make tiny metal splinters which, no matter how careful I am, end up sticking into my hands and making cuts that take a long time to heal.

In spite of everything, we keep moving along across the Indian Ocean. Every problem brings us closer to Sydney, the end of the first leg of the journey; in itself, a pilgrimage worthy of the name.

Saturday, November 10.

I awoke suddenly, feeling something change in the rhythm of *Manureva,* to find the sails aback. It was the beginning of a day during which the boat was difficult to handle, having a tendency to jibe constantly.

I now have all the instructions passed on to me by R.T.L. concerning my unruly Decca automatic pilot. I hauled down all sails and, taking advantage of a sunny day, set to work: removing and changing the cap, tightening screws and bolts, and so forth. The work took most of the morning. I used a line to tie myself to the stern and was in water up to my waist. To waterproof my oilskins I used tape to seal them to my boots, and I was able to putter around with the Decca without getting soaked.

I also disassembled, cleaned, and greased the roller of the mainsail before hoisting it.

Finally, I went below to change and had a cup of tea to warm me up.

During the past week—my ninth at sea—I've covered 1,510 nautical miles. My general average has increased and is now 179.2 miles per day, for an average speed of about 7.5 knots.

The albatrosses that have been escorting me now land on

the boat and come to within a few yards of me. They've become very much at ease in my presence.

When I finished all the repairs on the boat, I fixed myself a small meal by way of self-repair. I was just having my dessert when there was an enormous uproar from the cockpit. I rushed out—to find a mollymawk at the helm. I surmised that the mollymawk (a kind of albatross) had crashed into the mizzenmast or into a halyard, and then plunged into the cockpit. It seemed to have then become entangled in the steering mechanism and was unable to free itself. It was a fairly large bird—its wingspan was at least ten feet—and I knew that its beak was a dangerous weapon, and one that it knew how to use. I had heard stories about these birds from Cape Horn sailors at Saint-Malo. I didn't dare come too close; and yet, I didn't dare leave the bird there for very long. Then, by some miracle, the mollymawk succeeded in freeing itself without any help from me, jumped up on the side of the cockpit, climbed onto the rear deck, and from there launched itself into the air.

According to my calculations, in the past two weeks I've covered 3,000 miles; that is, an average of 220 to 230 nautical miles per day. That is a definitive break through the famous "wall" of 200 miles per day solo average; the wall that Chichester tried to cross in 1968, in his last *Gypsy Moth*. It was left to *Manureva* to succeed—and to succeed in the "roaring forties." That fact makes up for a lot of the problems and unpleasantness of the past couple of weeks.

I am still about 2,500 nautical miles off Sydney, although, thanks to the radiotelephone, I have already spoken with Australia, by way of Perth. Perth was the first Australian city I saw in 1966, when I emigrated aboard a French freighter to try my luck "down under." Perth was our first port-of-call, and it is therefore my first memory of Australia. I would like it to be the first place to hear me announce my arrival. (So much for symbolism.) It's hard to believe that so many years have passed since then; years in which much water has passed under the keel, so to speak, and years during which the extraordinary world of the sea has opened up to me.

Sunday, November 11.

A bad day at sea, with a series of jibes and damage to sails following a violent squall. Between squalls, I sit in the cockpit and read, only raising my eyes occasionally to watch the ballet of the albatrosses as they hover at the surface of the water and then rise after snacking on the algae there. It is, after all, Sunday: a day of rest, and, moreover, a day for celebrating victories.

Monday, November 12.

The weather last night was very strange. Squall followed squall till dawn—a very dubious dawn, in which dirty yellows contrasted sadly with pinks and blacks.

The entire morning was spent steering. We greeted the arrival of violent gusts of wind (up to fifty knots) by jibing. There was no indication on the barometer of anything unusual.

Before lunch, a spell of comparative calm gave me time to run up the mainsail, although it took me a good half hour because the slides are sticking so badly. I have worked hard enough to deserve a meal, and I'm pleased to be able to eat it in peace.

After doing a tape for R.T.L., I reached my family in France. One by one, they took turns talking to me. Mama was pleased when I told her that I had just finished eating the *pigeon aux champignons* that she had made for me. I talked to Jeff about technical problems, of course, and added more items to the list of things I need. He assured me that what I had asked for previously was ready, and that they had gone over the problem of the slides very carefully. He is certain that I must expect some breakage no matter what kind I use.

Our connection was remarkably clear, and I felt as though I were sitting in the room with my whole family. So much so that I was reluctant to end the conversation. We talked for twenty minutes.

Tuesday, November 13.

I've broken my own solo record, the 10,000-mile trek from Réunion to France in sixty-six days. Today is my sixty-seventh day at sea, and on this voyage I've already covered 11,000 miles.

I am still at 43°S (and 102°10′E). The sky is gray once more and a fine rain is falling. It is time for caution. I took in a reef, and then another one, in the mainsail. Even so, I know that it is foolhardy for me to continue with so much sail.

After a three-hour struggle with myself, I decided to haul down the mainsail. After a one-hour struggle with the winch, I got it down. It was just in time. A series of strong gusts came along to justify my intuition. If I may use an expression inappropriate to the walls of water around me, I was playing with fire by hesitating so long.

It was a very dark night. *Manureva,* under her single jib, moved bravely along at her customary ten knots. In these fearsome waves, it requires at least partial insanity to have even the jib's 236 square feet aloft. But, waves or not and insane or not, it was a good night.

Wednesday, November 14.

Fog, spray, and drizzle, as always in these miserable latitudes.

I spent the day working on the mainsail and the mizzen, until I was ready to drop from exhaustion.

At about 1900, just as I was preparing a cup of hot tea, I heard a siren! Rushing out on deck, I saw, aft to starboard, *Australian Endeavour,* a container-cargo, coming alongside. After many hand signals and the customary exchange of flags, I rushed to the radio for a contact on frequency 2182 (the distress frequency). The ship had put out of Liverpool three weeks before, en route to Melbourne. The captain offered to pass on any messages that I might have and he also gave me my position: 43°03′S, 109°19′E. We were 550 miles south-southwest of Cape Leeuwin and 150 miles from its longitude—which coincided, within fifteen miles, with my own calculations.I am rather proud of having come so close.

This encounter, the first that I have had for so long, especially coming as it did after all those terrible and exhausting days and nights, was an extraordinary tonic for me. It made me feel that I was reborn into a world inhabited by warm, friendly creatures whose membership in the human race I shared. There are moments when my need for solidarity, the group instinct, the need to belong, becomes so intense that it feels as though I were melted into the species. I don't believe that a hermit flees the human race. I know from my own experience, as a hermit of the sea, that one is never so close to humanity as when one is alone.

The men who had just spoken to me of the joys of living on *terra firma* were soon lost in the fog and the darkness. They took with them, unwittingly, my escort of mollymawks and albatrosses that had been following me since the Cape of Good Hope. The birds obviously preferred the ship to my little boat. Of my winged friends, only one albatross remains with me: an old and slightly decrepit bird whose feathers seem to come ungiued with every gust of wind, revealing his whitish down. There are also a couple of black birds that look remarkably like crows.

Thursday, November 15.

I'm beginning a new logbook, one with a red cover, to record my sixty-ninth day at sea.

I've now crossed the longitude of Cape Leeuwin, the southern cape which follows Good Hope on the around-the-world route of the tall ships. We have left the Indian Ocean and are in the "Southern Ocean" of the Australians. I have set a course for Bass Strait, which separates the island of Tasmania from the Australian mainland. From there, it will be 500 miles to Sydney.

At this point, I must say that *Manureva* is truly an extraordinary boat, a "performance" boat designed for speed and specially fitted for very difficult conditions. The records set, the speeds reached—all these things are, after all, to be expected of *Manureva,* given the way she was built and the years of careful preparation and planning that went into her. One thing worries me. How am I to know whether I've used *Manureva* to her maximum potential? Have I made the best possible use of her in difficult waters? In other words, have I met my personal goals?

The past three days saw me hit rock bottom. I felt that I was alone and lost at the farthest reaches of the world, in a nightmare of fog, almost permanent drizzle, violent squalls, an enormous swell, and incredible winds. I have to keep telling myself that I am here because I want to be; that nothing forces me to be here; that I can always escape simply by setting a course northward. After all, I remind myself, I am not going to spend my life here. I am only passing through. What about all the sailors in the last century who did spend their lives in these waters, under these skies that remained gray for months on end? They must have belonged to another race of men, a stouter race, to endure it.

The fog today is a bit less dense than yesterday, but navigation remains difficult and the sea is still rough. I may be getting used to it. In any event, things are going more smoothly since I've accepted the fact that I must reduce sail sooner rather than later. It does not pay to rub the ocean the wrong way.

A sudden barometric drop made me haul down the mizzen in a hurry. Later, I took a wave broadside—a lesson that it is much better to let the waves carry us.

Friday, November 16.

The fog and drizzle are not heavy enough this morning to conceal the solid walls of water moving crossways around *Manureva,* and we will content ourselves with being carried.

Toward noon, the sun was out briefly, touching the enormous swells with eerie light (there must have been a gigantic storm somewhere at this latitude) and giving me a heaven-sent opportunity to whip out my sextant. My position: 41°27′S, 117°20′E.

I ran up the mizzen and let out the reefs in the mainsail before hoisting the genoa. I then opened the hatch to air out the cabin. Finally, I bailed out the bottom—about five quarts of water. Then I settled down to wait for evening, at peace for once.

The sky at sunset was an inverted bowl of pink, purple, and yellow. I could not resist filming it to have a record of it for my friends.

The wind fell to zero. I hauled down the jib and was in bed by 2000. The alarm clock was set for midnight.

Saturday, November 17.

The night, for once, was longer than I had planned. I did not hear the alarm and slept through, without waking, until 0600! I scrambled on deck to get under way before hoisting the reaching jib, and then busied myself with various little repair jobs—more out of the need to placate a guilty conscience than for any other reason.

I spent most of the afternoon trying to get the Decca pilot working again. There was a breeze, but it was too weak for the Gianoli pilot, and its antenna was not sensitive enough to be activated. The boat luffed, then jibed; but I don't think that I have any right to complain. I've had sunlight since yesterday, and to me that is worth all the wind in the world.

The week's tally shows that I've traveled 1,491 miles. The total mileage thus far is 12,289 miles. Daily average: 182.5 miles. Average speed: 7.6 knots. That is really moving.

I had a very good radio contact with R.T.L. yesterday. Today, an equally good session with my family. They are getting ready for their flight to Sydney. I was able to tell them about the week and about my experiences in the "roaring forties."

For the past week, I've been maintaining *Manureva's* course at the same latitude despite the temptation to head northward. The reason is that the further south we sail, the shorter the distance, since the diameter of the earth is smaller the nearer we approach the pole. There have been a few nice days without the furious Niagaras that I encountered when first entering the Indian Ocean. Those days have been useful in restoring both the boat and the skipper to working condition. I have gotten into the habit of reefing as soon as the wind rises. I reduce my sail; yet I know for a fact that I'm going to have a certain amount of damage no matter how careful I am. I simply accept the inevitability of having to make repairs as soon as the wind drops again. Undoubtedly, *Manureva* will begin to show a few weak points now. After all, she has over 11,000 miles under her keel. I no longer try to keep up as much sail as possible as long as possible. I have developed a more gentle philosophy: I keep my hand in by trying to maintain a more or less constant speed to keep up my average.

I have gone back over the 2,000 miles that I've just crossed. On the chart, drawn as a straight line, it indeed turns out to be 2,000 miles. But in reality, drawn from one meridian point to the next, the distance is much longer; because sometimes I headed south, and sometimes north in order to get away from the Antarctic ice. So much for the 200-mile-per-day record that Sir Francis Chichester tried to break in 1969 with the specially built *Gypsy Moth V*. Sir Francis's purpose was to cover 4,000 nautical miles in twenty days by taking advantage of the trade winds between Africa and Central America. He was unable to do so, despite favorable weather and excellent equipment. Now, if we measure a straight line from the Cape of Good Hope to Cape Leeuwin, we find that it is 4,300 nautical miles—which I've covered in less than twenty-two days. And, if we measure from meridian point to meridian point, we find that I've actually covered 4,500 miles in that time.

My pleasure in breaking that record is enhanced by recalling the words of Sir Francis himself after his failure to do so in 1969: "In my opinion," he said, "when the record is finally broken, it will be broken by a multihulled boat."

My interior barometer is now in harmony with actual meteorological conditions. I think that I will be in Sydney in about ten days, though I would not try to fix an exact date at this point. Weather conditions along the coast are more variable than in the open sea, where weather systems can develop without interference.

I've been at sea for over two months, and I have been able to get down to essentials. I realize that, for me, family ties are the most important thing in the world, and I am eager to see my family once more and to see Teura, who is also going to meet me in Australia. Whenever the weather permits, I do not hesitate to run up as much sail as possible—as much for the sake of speed as for the sake of seeing my loved ones as soon as I can. It is not only a question of breaking or setting records. It is just as important to me to know, as I've already said, that I've lived up to the goals I set for myself—that I've fought as good a fight as I could in the circumstances. To satisfy myself on that point, I asked to be radioed information on the positions of the racing boats that have left the Cape of Good Hope for Sydney. Once I have that information, I'll be able to calculate their averages and compare them to my own. I am eager to see how they are affected by the wind and the sea in the Indian Ocean. In those contrary swells, those giant waves, the fog and the rain and the squalls, I suspect that a conventional sailing vessel with a crew will have an easier time of it than a solo sailor. Even so, it will certainly not be easy for them, and I am eager to see how their speed compares with mine.

Sunday, November 18.

Really beautiful weather, and I am greeting it by spreading all my damp clothing in the cockpit to dry.

I've been in radio contact with Denis Wolanski in Sydney. We've known each other for years; and it is good, after a long absence, to relax in the warmth of a friend's voice again.

The sea is calm, and I am resting and relaxing today. I've

lashed the tiller and settled down to read. It is Sunday, and I like days of rest now and then. The end of the day was made perfect by the appearance, after dark, of a spectacularly illuminated cargo ship, like a fairy castle drifting silently in the night.

Monday, November 19; Tuesday, November 20;
Wednesday, November 21.

For the past three days it has been relatively calm and I have had only the usual small navigation problems, accompanied of course by the usual repair chores. I did have a red-letter day: I managed to contact Teura, in Tahiti, via Sydney Radio.

It is fortunate that the weather has been fairly good, because I have not been feeling very well since Monday. I seem to be progressively more exhausted, and my reflexes have begun to slow down. I have tried doses of vitamins, thus far with no discernible effect. On Tuesday afternoon, in fact, I had to lie down. That night, I forced myself to eat although I had no appetite.

Wednesday morning I awoke at 0300. My joints were sore and I was as weak as a limp rag. I felt as though I had just finished a particularly grueling rugby match. It was not until Wednesday night, when I was awakened by the alarm, that I finally discovered the reason for these strange bouts of intense weakness and debilitation. I was being slowly asphyxiated by carbon monoxide fumes—the same stupid accidental asphyxiation that you read about when a family is found dead in their apartment because their stove or furnace is not properly vented.

The alarm is what saved me. I had enclosed myself completely in the cabin because there were squalls and a rough sea, and I was trying to spare myself any unpleasant surprises during the few hours of precious sleep that I allowed myself. It took an enormous effort for me to drag myself to the cockpit and open the hatch. The fumes from the generator accumulated in the cabin through a series of coincidences and malfunctions (a breakdown in the cooling circuit) and if I had not awakened when I did, I feel certain that I would not have been alive the next morning. I had absolutely no idea that anything was wrong; and I was already so weak that I don't think it would have taken much more to finish me off. I could hardly walk, there was a loud ringing in my ears, and I was suffering from an intense nausea which left me totally exhausted.

For the next thirty-six hours, I was in misery. I could barely move, and every movement of my arms or legs required an extraordinary effort of will. To make an adjustment in the sail meant that I had to sit down to rest every few minutes; and it seemed that every maneuver took an eternity to accomplish.

In short, my "record breaking" almost turned into "the incomplete crossing." During those three days, the rhythm of the boat was entirely disrupted, and I lost about thirty-six hours of sailing time.

Thursday, November 22.

I am still not feeling well, and the barometer is falling rapidly. I've hoisted the running jib, and even that small chore has left me totally exhausted.

We jibed several times. Once more, several slides on the mainsail broke and I hauled down the sail to make repairs. It seemed the hardest job that I've ever had to do. During the afternoon I fell into bed and slept for three hours.

Friday, November 23.

It seems that it is becoming harder and harder for me to move around and I'm weak as a baby. It goes without saying that I'm extremely eager to get to shore. I haven't seen land since we passed the Canaries—12,000 miles ago. I am trying to get to the various little repair jobs that are necessary for me to be able to maneuver well when I do land.

I am surprised, and not a little worried, that I haven't seen any ships since sighting *Australian Endeavour*.

My position, 38°55′S, 141°43′E, is now about thirty nautical miles from Cape Nelson and ninety miles from Cape Otway. The depth finder showed the bottom at 700 feet at 1300. At 1500, it was 505 feet; at 1600, 370 feet. At 1655, I shouted for joy: 135 feet! Then I wept, partly from excitement, partly from exhaustion, partly from anticipation.

At 2100 we rounded Cape Otway and I was finally able to make out, far off to port, the lights of several freighters.

I have four days left to reach Sydney within the time I've allotted myself and to equal the average time of the clipper ships.

Saturday, November 24.

I am feeling a bit better, though I'm still far from well.

The winds have now shifted to the south. I let out the reefs and, an hour later, ran up the jib. The sea is still calm and is beginning to look inhabited: freighters, cruisers—and hundreds of dark-colored birds.

I am at the end of my week. From meridian point to meridian point, I've covered 1,299 nautical miles. My total is 14,079 miles since leaving Saint-Malo, for a daily average of 182.8 miles. Not bad.

But I'm not there yet.

Sunday, November 25.

It's very depressing to be becalmed when I'm so close to my goal. I tried to get under way at 0600, and then went back to bed. I still do not feel well.

By noon, I could no longer see the Hogan Islands or the Wilson Promontory. I think that we've now passed through the Bass Strait and that we're back in the Tasman Sea and the immensities of the Pacific.

I sighted two off-shore drilling platforms and came quite close to both. There were a number of men on the platforms, but no one waved.

Later, I encountered a mass of lumber lashed together and populated by a colony of seals. At that point, the water was too deep for me to get a reading.

The barometer is falling and the setting sun is an orange ball surrounded by a pale halo. I see lightning to port.

I seem to have regained my appetite and I've fixed myself a large helping of rice *aux oignons,* the specialty of the house.

I have a feeling of nostalgia as I draw nearer to Sydney. The city has played an important part in my life. It was there that I became involved with the sea. Pensive, and perhaps a bit melancholy in the evocation of those not-too-distant years, I have been sitting in the cockpit for a long while, thinking about the various stages by which the young French student who got off the ship at Sydney was transformed into the seaman who is now on a solo cruise around the world.

Clamecy, Dijon, Paris, Sydney—all stops on my first trip around the world of youthful uncertainties until, unsuspecting, I found the road that eventually led to my greatest adventure.

I had gone to Sydney in search of the sun and I found the sea instead. That may sound dramatic—but it is not quite true. The truth is that I've always loved the water. At home, at Clamecy, we had the Yonne River where I learned to swim at a very early age and where I learned to handle a small sailboat, a pleasure that eventually became a necessity. Later, studying English as a student in Paris (after a brief stopover in Dijon), I found a security blanket at Bullier, the student swimming pool. Then I discovered boat racing. With my friends in Clamecy, we started a racing club. One of the good things about being a student is that you have a lot of free time. At the end of the school year, I was able to devote the summer months to my new passion. I was completely absorbed in it and was busy raising money, renting a workshop, building boats, recruiting members for the club—all of it in preparation for what was to come.

It was not that I did not enjoy Paris and my studies. I did indeed. I loved my work there, and I loved the intellectual gymnastics involved in working with words. It has always seemed to me that to take words from one language and render them in another language is a creative act. I had chosen English as my field of study because of a natural inclination toward that language, and also because it was the field in which, until then, I had shown the most ability.

Even so, I felt the need for something more. At first I thought that it was only a matter of my missing something—something physical: the sun, the open air, the freedom of the outdoors. I was not the only student at the Sorbonne studying English, and the classrooms were so crowded sometimes that I had to follow a lecture as best I could while standing in the hallway. There were simply too many people for me to be comfortable. A fine situation for a young man who had come to Paris in search of an education!

Paradoxically, I also suffered from solitude. I was to spend months alone on the sea in later life. As a student, however, I could never mingle with the crowds on the Boulevard Saint-Michel or join the mobs on the Paris subway without feeling the most intense isolation, as though I were a lost child. It is a

109

feeling familiar to anyone who chooses to live in solitude for a period of time in order to find himself by recognizing his dependence on other people and thus becoming closer to them. It was in Paris, in the midst of a crowd, that I lost contact with other human beings. There were times when I remained in my room for days at a time, making my meals from a supply of groceries that I had laid in to last for a week.

One morning, the whole thing was brought to a head by the sun. Or rather, by the fact that I could not see the sun because of the apartment buildings outside my window. I suddenly realized that if I lived in a city I would never have the pleasure of looking up at the sky. And if I did look up, the chances were that I would see nothing more than a gray dome overhead. It was not enough to be able to swim in a pool, or to shoot down the streams of central France whenever I managed to get away. The dream of a trip around the world began to germinate in Paris; and there were three of us who shared that dream.

I had left the University of Dijon with two friends who also wanted to study in Paris. I don't know which one of us first had the idea of the "bread truck," as we called it—the kind of van that has since become so popular among young people. The bread truck was going to be our means of transportation on our travels along the highways of the planet. We were entirely serious about the plan. We attended all the explorers' lectures at the Salle Pleyel in Paris. And whenever we saw a van on the street—usually a Volkswagen or a Land Rover— we stopped to examine it at length, often getting down on our knees to examine the suspension system. I was already at work with my maps, tracing our first itinerary. I am not sure what had inspired us. Perhaps it was nothing more than the subconscious desire of three young men to prolong our schoolboy days as long as possible before facing "real life." Or it may have been a vague perception of the call of the open sea.

I do not come from a seafaring family, and I do not think that there was any longing for the sea at that time. I think that the sun itself was enough to give me ideas of journeys to distant lands.

The first job, obviously, was to put my family in the proper frame of mind to listen to my plans for travel. That is not easy in a closely knit family, which takes a very dim view of long separations. And my friends and I planned to be away at least two years.

I began, deviously enough, on a rather oblique psychological tack: I suggested that my English studies would be helped enormously if I traveled to English-speaking countries. It was in this context that Australia was first mentioned, since it is an English-speaking country—and since it is conveniently located at the other end of the world.

A dream is like a fragile vase. If you discuss it and handle it too much, it is likely to be destroyed. We discussed, delayed, discussed some more; and then the workaday world intervened. My friends had problems with their studies; and then they had to worry about their military service. So, I was left alone with the dream. Far from being discouraged, I was absolutely certain that I would die if I had to remain in France.

At the beginning of this book, I mentioned how my father had taught me never to give up, and how, thanks to him, I had learned that dreams have a way of being translated into reality. It was a happy coincidence, therefore, that it was my father who clipped an advertisement, in English, from *Le Monde* and sent it to me. The ad described a position that was available in the Faculty of Letters in Sydney, Australia. A position as "lecturer." In my innocence, I thought that a "lecturer" was a teaching assistant, a position for which I might hope to qualify. This seemed the perfect opportunity to get to Australia and, at the same time, to perfect my knowledge of English. I could not pass it up. I sent out my application immediately and then settled down to wait. I heard nothing. I then decided not to wait any longer: I would go to Australia and apply in person. Therefore, I booked passage on a ship sailing from Marseilles on December 26.

A few days before that date, I received a letter from Australia declining my services as a lecturer. But it was too late. I had decided to take my chances. The day after Christmas, my family put me aboard a freighter that, after a series of ports-of-call, via Suez and the East Indies, would eventually reach Australia. Not being altogether irresponsible, I took advantage of every port-of-call along the way to dispatch an avalanche of letters to colleges, institutes, and universities in Australia, offering my services. I had also, in conspiracy with English-speaking friends, concocted an irresistible letter to the head of the French Department at the University of Sydney, explaining that, while I understood that the position for which I had applied might already be filled, I hoped to be allowed to call on him when I arrived in Australia, for a session of job-counselling.

I also had an ace in the hole: boats. I had received a teaching certificate from the National Institute of Sports, and I hoped to be able to get a job as an instructor. I had letters of commendation attesting to my skill in paddle-racing; for I hoped, whatever happened, to be able to continue to enjoy my favorite sport. Nor had I forgotten my diving tanks, a tent, or anything that I might need to snare a few fish along the coast, provided that my welcome in Australia was at least moderately warm. Of course, I could not travel without my books and technical dictionaries, just in case I wrangled a few translations; or without a skillet and a stew pan, being a Frenchman. All told, my baggage weighed at least 600 or 700 pounds.

When we arrived in Sydney I was a bit uneasy about leaving the ship. I had been fascinated by everything aboard, and I had been more or less adopted by the crew. My fears were groundless. From the moment I set foot ashore, I met with nothing but warmth and friendliness. A customs officer tapped me on the shoulder, welcomed me to his country, and offered to take charge of my luggage so that, while I was calling at the University, I would not have to pay for storage.

I immediately visited the University and called on the head of the French Department. The interview went very well indeed. We understood each other, as people sometimes do from the very first moment. But, more than that, I had an advantage over other applicants for the job who had written from France. I was neither a photograph nor a resumé, but flesh and blood, sitting in the chairman's office and answering his questions directly. Also, I represented an economy: I was already in Australia, and the University would have to pay the travel expenses of any other French applicant who might be hired. Therefore I got the job.

I still did not know that a lecturer was a full-fledged teacher. I thought that I was going to be an assistant. In fact, I did not discover that there had been a misunderstanding until I was issued a small yellow button which, it was explained to me, was given only to lecturers and which allowed that privileged rank access to virtually every part of the University. My suspicion that something had gone wrong somewhere was confirmed when, shortly thereafter, the nature of my duties was explained to me in detail. The gods obviously had decided to give me my big chance.

The University, in opening its doors to me, offered me an opportunity that had nothing to do with my duties as a teacher. For the first time in my life, I was going to live on the seashore. And what a shore it was. Sydney is an astonishing city, with countless inlets from a bay which would be difficult to describe without multiplying adjectives and adverbs unduly. Suffice it to say that I had constantly before my eyes an incredible spectacle of sailing vessels in constant motion; sailing was the pastime and the passion of a people fascinated by water sports. For me, at first, before I knew sailing, the boats were a seascape rather than a passion. For the moment, I was content to watch the colorful sails as they weaved their way majestically through the ferryboats and the commercial vessels, a kaleidoscopic vision which was itself an invitation to faraway places.

The Sydney Canoe Club was a half-day's journey from the campus and, for that reason, I did not go as often as I would have liked. One day, however, some of my faculty colleagues asked me to join them for a sail. One of their crew was unable to get away, and they needed a replacement in the race. I accepted and, for the first time, I set foot on a sailing vessel. That was in 1966. I was twenty-two years old at the time. And, on that day, sailing struck me like a thunderbolt. I knew at once that sailing was not only an interesting and exciting sport, but also a mysterious society of initiates with its own language to protect it from the profane; a language that had an evocative power fortified by the magic of actions born of words. It was also a marvelous way of handling time and space. I understood immediately that if I could learn to handle this boat—which, at that moment, was cutting proudly through the waves of the bay of Sydney—I would be able, one day, to take a boat to those same faraway lands that had been the object of my dreams as a student in a Parisian garret. By learning to sail, I would learn not only the rules and the discipline of another sport, but I would also make it possible to transform my dreams into reality. The old dream of a trip around the world with my two friends would be realized—not in a "bread truck," but on a sleek sailboat that would allow me to push back ever farther the line of the horizon.

My excitement on that first sail was irrepressible. Every time I saw a boat on the bay, I asked my friends how much it cost. Then I quickly computed how many hours I would have to spend tutoring and how many translations I would have to do in order to buy it. My tour of the world had started its Siren Song; this time with a vengeance.

That evening, as soon as I got back to the campus, even before going home, I visited the library and took out every book on sailing and sailboats that I could find. Then, first sitting next to the open window in the room, enjoying the night air, and later stretched out on my bed till dawn, I underwent my preliminary literary initiation into the language and techniques of yachting. It was the first time, but hardly the last, that sailing made me spend a sleepless night. I was supposed to sail again with my friends the following Sunday—in a race, no less—and I felt I owed it to myself and to them to know as much as I could. And, although I began by being astonished that sailors were not allowed to refer to a rope as a rope, I was soon able to talk about "lines" and "halyards," to say nothing of sheets and jibs, with the best of them.

Canoe racing had undoubtedly predisposed me to the spirit of competition, for within a few days I had learned enough to become a useful member of the crew. In racing, you learn in a few outings what pleasure-sailing takes years to teach. Racing requires absolutely unwavering attention so that, when you are already going fast, you can go even faster. It demands that, at the very moment that you think you've found the ideal trim, you start adjusting the sails again. It requires endless repetition until every movement, every series of maneuvers practiced against a stop-watch, is perfect.

Everything that I learned in Australia was put to the test later elsewhere. But then, Australians sail year-round. For every ten races held in France during a season, there are at least fifty in Australia. In fact, during my first year in that country, there was a minor uprising of skippers' wives demanding that there be at least one Sunday a month without a race, so that their husbands could do things around the house.

115

I spent four seasons—that is, two years, since there is a winter championship as well as a summer championship—learning the secrets of sailing. I soon became impatient with regattas—that is, races around triangular courses marked by buoys—and felt the urge to strike out on the open sea. I was able to sign onto ocean-going yachts, and there I felt at home. The old dream of going around the world to see places and to learn about people continued to haunt me. I applied myself to learning the techniques of sailing on the open sea with the idea that I was practicing for an adventure that lay in the future.

But I knew that I had to go beyond mere learning. I found a place among the crew on a racing boat by answering an ad. I explained that I was French, and that, in addition to being an able-bodied seaman, I could also cook! The prestige of French cuisine serves many unexpected ends. (This detail was later taken up by newspapers, for lack of more substantial news, and transformed into an amusing anecdote.)

Thus, when Eric Tabarly came to Australia with his *Pen Duick III* to take part in the famous Sydney–Hobart Race, I became known as "the other Frenchman" in the race. I was a bona fide member of the crew of one of the yachts registered for that great classic; and that, for me, was a definite step up in my career on the sea, for to be a crewman was an eagerly sought prize and a prestigious one. The morning of the race, there were about sixty young men wandering along the dock, their packs slung over their shoulders, waiting and hoping that, at the last moment, some crew member would not show up and would have to be replaced. The Sydney–Hobart in Australia overshadows even the Davis Cup—and that in a country where tennis is taken very seriously indeed.

It was on this occasion that I first met my famous compatriot, Eric Tabarly. After the race, part of Eric's crew returned to France. And, since there was a place aboard *Pen Duick III,*

116

I signed on. As it turned out, that simple decision marked a turning point in my life.

There were five of us aboard on that memorable cruise. We were surprised by a hurricane off New Caledonia, and we survived only because we did everything that had to be done. It was not as easy as it may sound. I have seen rougher seas since then, but never have I experienced winds as violent as those. There is a saying that seamen are made by storms. I might add that storms also forge bonds among seamen.

The events that followed that cruise back to France follow a logical, though not necessarily obvious, sequence: a year "off" to resume my studies; my arrival in Paris in May 1968, when the paving stones were flying and youngsters were determined to force liberty, equality, and fraternity down the throats of everyone else; my decision to breathe once more the serene air of the sea; Eric's presence at Lorient, preparing *Pen Duick IV* for the Transatlantic Race in June; and the fact that he was shorthanded at the moment. Then, everything began to happen faster: *Pen Duick's* collision in the Channel and her subsequent dropping out of the race; the repair of the boat; the Atlantic crossing followed by the setting of a new record for the Transpacific; Eric's decision to sell *Pen Duick IV;* my acquisition of it by borrowing the money; the return to France by completing an around-the-world cruise that gave me the experience necessary to win the 1972 Transatlantic.

And now, the old *Pen Duick IV,* transformed into *Manureva,* the companion of my travels, was about to win new laurels in the wake of the great clipper ships of the nineteenth century.

But I am counting my chickens before they hatch. There are still miles ahead of us, and it is never safe to anticipate, at sea even less than on land.

117

Monday, November 26.

Here, at least, the barometer can be relied on.

A sudden gust of thirty-five knots caused *Manureva* to jibe; but, since there is some good in everything bad, I took advantage of it to begin bearing to port toward Sydney—while taking a tally of the usual damage: broken battens in the mainsail and the mizzen.

The sea is rough, and a strong current is braking *Manureva*'s speed. That is usual in these parts. It is the "southerly set," a current that is the torment of participants in the Sydney–Hobart Race.

I've been tied up on the radio with interviews, which began as soon as I raised Sydney. But, during the afternoon, I set the spinnaker; and, from that time on, there was no time for anything but staying at the helm.

It is only 150 miles to the Heads, the promontories that form the bay of Sydney; but the waves are unimpressed. One of them has thoroughly drenched the captain, and a halyard has broken.

During the evening, I ran up the reaching jib after spending an hour trying to haul down the spinnaker, which was dragging. And then, after giving the matter some more thought, I brought down the reaching jib and ran up the running jib.

I should be about twenty-five miles from Jervis Bay, which is about eighty-five miles from Sydney. I therefore have about 110 nautical miles to go—about eleven hours, if all goes well.

Tuesday, November 27.

I am now on a course perpendicular to the coast, after spending the night following in the wakes of freighters to such an extent that I had no need to take soundings.

I did take a sounding this morning at 0900: 977 feet. After that, I remained in the cockpit.

Then things began to happen very quickly. There were occasional strong gusts of wind; the clouds were low in the sky, and visibility was practically zero. It was raining steadily, and even the palms of my hands were wet, though they had been glued to the helm for a long time. Then, suddenly I saw something dark and unmoving ahead—the sharp silhouette of the North Head to starboard. We were only fifteen miles away. It was precisely at 1020 that *Manureva* and I, riding on the waves and covered with foam, passed the Heads and entered the bay of Sydney.

I saw a small fleet of motorboats and sailboats rushing out of a small bay to port to greet me. Boats of every kind had been waiting for me, and, when *Manureva* rose on the crest of a wave, I saw my family on one of them. By then, the boats had surrounded me; but I was going so fast that they had trouble keeping up. Nonetheless, we waved and shouted back and forth.

In my mind I was going over my figures as I watched the familiar Australian shore, adding 561 miles to last week's total. I have a grand total of 14,640 nautical miles in seventy-nine days. That is, 185 miles per day at an average speed of 7.7 knots. It was a new solo record; but it was, above all, equal to the time of *Cutty Sark* a century earlier.

I reached Sydney surrounded by friends and overwhelmed by the warmth of their affectionate welcome. I felt simultaneously the humility of the pilgrim returning to the sources of his faith, and great pride in having done what I set out to do.

It would be difficult to overemphasize the contrast between my welcome in the bay of Sydney and that on another coast, one Friday in July 1972. On that day, I crossed the finish-line of the Transatlantic sitting in my cockpit, so tired that I could not budge, unable to handle the sails, tears of joy and fatigue running down my cheeks, the boat left to herself to do whatever she wanted to do. There was no one waiting for me that day. ("We were expecting a schooner this weekend," I was told by a fisherman I met at the entrance to the bay.) I was astonished to see neither boat nor airplane—nothing that I had been led to expect by accounts that I had read. Finally, a single small airplane appeared in the distance and circled overhead twice before returning whence it had come. It was Lelouch, looking for his *Vendredi 13,* accompanied by his brother, who had just figured out that that strange white spot on the water below could only be me. The dark silhouette of land beyond my bow began to rise in the water as we went forward in the fog and the heat. Gradually, like a veiled red disc, the sun appeared and became the only witness to my victory before sinking slowly, gently, behind the hills of Newport.

Later, of course, there was celebration: boats hurrying to meet me, horns and whistles blowing, planes zooming overhead, reporters swarming to ask questions and demand explanations, laughter, shouts—all the things that serve as distractions and shorten that moment of overwhelming joy, that second of intense pleasure which, however ephemeral it may be, justifies and completes twenty days, thirteen hours, and five minutes of bitter struggle.

This morning in the bay of Sydney, my parents and friends had waited in the cold and drizzle. Now, they formed a proud escort for my aluminum bird at the far end of another ocean. In Newport, the sun had shown itself to compensate for the missing crowd. Here, the warmth of human hearts more than compensated for the coldness of the morning air.

As soon as I had entered Bass Strait, rounding the southern coast of Australia, I knew that I would not sleep again until I reached Sydney. Victory is won at the price of a final, all-out effort. At the same time, I began to feel a kind of exhilaration brought on by the anticipation of seeing my family and friends again in Sydney and also by memories. Yes, memories of day after day of work and worry, of anxiety and solitude. Now, the sea had brought us to a safe port; to a haven of calm, security, and peace.

And so, escorted by friends, family, and memories, I arrived. I tried to haul down the mainsail—and it stuck. Once more, I shinnied up the mast with my hammer, tapping here and tapping there, trying desperately to overcome the last obstacle that separated me from what I had dreamed about so many times: a boiling hot shower.

5

The waiting, the anguish

Saturday, December 29.

Today, at 1800, the fourteen remaining participants in the Whitbread Race will begin the third round of their competition by sailing across the South Pacific and the Southern Sea to Rio, "leaving Cape Horn to port," according to the laconic expression of their instructions.

I will leave one hour later and escort them to the same rendezvous with glory before our routes separate and *Manureva* and I continue on a straight course to Saint-Malo in order to complete our loop around the world.

For almost everyone involved, with the exception of perhaps two or three people, this leg will be the solemn moment which will make of us, simple seamen that we are, knights of the sea with the title, "Cape Horners." It is a gratuitous title, but a prestigious one nonetheless, evoking as it does so many dreams and so much magic.

I left Sydney harbor on schedule, at 1900, heading out between North Head and South Head on a tranquil sea. The

123

temperature was ideal; the wind gentle from the north-north-east. Then I turned due east.

Around midnight, I had proof, if I needed any, that my thirty-two days in Sydney had not caused me to rust unduly. *Manureva* overtook *Adventure,* which was running second on corrected time during the first two stages of the race, behind *Sayula II* but ahead of my compatriots aboard *Kriter* and *Grand Louis* who were two hours behind *Adventure.* They were a day ahead of *Guia.* After 14,000 miles, the closeness of their positions gave some indication of the quality of the racers and of the kind of race that this stage would be.

Despite the circumstances of our departure, which reminded me of a ship leaving on a cruise of the South Seas with a load of tourists, a thought occurred to me that sent a shiver down my spine: On November 19, *Tauranga* lost a man overboard in a storm and nothing could be done to save him. On November 24, Dominique Guillet, the skipper and the soul of *33 Export,* was swept overboard by a wave from the west. Since then, nothing has been quite the same.

The Indian Ocean has exacted its tribute and, in so doing, has marked each one of us. It may be because I am sailing alone, but, for some reason, these losses have affected me more than I would have thought possible. At the same time, I am convinced that nothing will ever keep the maritime racer from thinking that his only concern is simply to go faster and always faster, if possible without accidents, race or no race. And I know that no one will ever persuade him that this race is the insane undertaking of maniacs unaware of the danger involved and not obedience to a law as old as the world itself, compeling certain men to go further than anyone else has ever gone before.

The ocean also exacted another form of tribute, a technical tribute in this case, from most of the participants: torn sails, broken masts, damaged rudders, and much more. *Sayula* narrowly missed being lost forever in those icy, raging waters after a "knock down" that literally turned her upside down. By some miracle, she righted herself—dragging two of her crew through the water by their safety harnesses. The Indian Ocean is indeed a sea of troubles, and also of tragedy and of fear.

It is true that some of the participants reached Sydney only a few days ago, and that they've barely had time to lay in fresh supplies of food and water before setting out again. I, on the other hand, had all the time in the world to repair and prepare *Manureva* for the great encounter with Cape Horn. Still, it was not the most relaxing layover imaginable for me, since I had to work through the list of repairs and modifications to be done—a list that ran to twelve pages in my large notebook.

In appearance, *Manureva* is as ship-shape and proud now as she was when we first sailed from Saint-Malo; but in reality the upper works, on the whole, have suffered a good deal from being subjected almost constantly to extreme stress. Even so, only one yard of line out of 3,000 showed any sign of fatigue during our 14,000 miles; and then it was only because of really extreme conditions. In the final analysis, with the day-to-day repairs that I did, we reached port without any serious damage and even without too many near-misses.

Be that as it may, no boat is ever hauled without revealing a few unpleasant surprises. *Manureva* had to be repainted, of course, to smooth the bottom and so cut down on resistance through the water on the next leg of the voyage; and she had to be scraped down to remove the usual algae and other marine accumulations. But that was not all. The hull had been hammered by the waves, and the impact of these walls of water had left its mark here and there. There were times, in very high winds, when I had seen patches of paint blowing past me; but it was not until we were in port that I was able to see just how much damage had been done.

We also had to weld two cracks that had appeared at the spot where the beams are attached to the lateral floats. During this operation, we noticed that the entire forward part of these floats (which, fortunately, do not connect with the aft floats because of the different watertight compartments) was practically full of water. We had to bore a hole in the underside of the compartment to allow the water to drain so that the fissure could be soldered.

In other words, there was a great deal of work for me and my friends and family in Sydney. More than enough for those who had come from France and for those who lived in Australia. They had all come not only to offer congratulations, but also to offer a hand when needed. And chief among these, of course, was my brother Jean-François—Jeff—who had followed our struggle by radio and who got together everything that we needed in Australia.

At the Australian Cruising Yacht Club on Ruschcutter's Bay, everyone was tremendously busy. *Manureva,* only a few feet away from two of the boats from the Whitbread, had a joyous, excited team of workers hovering over her. It was the holiday season of 1973, the time for the trials for the Southern Cross Cup; a week of international races of which the most famous is the Sydney–Hobart Race. Australian sailing fans were even more excited about their own races than they were about the Whitbread or about "the other Frenchman" following in the wake of the clipper ships.

A group of very good friends were working along with the Colas clan:

Felix Aubry de La Noë, as good-natured as most seamen of Mediterranean stock, who had joined the crew of *Kriter* at Cape Town for the second stage of the Whitbread, and who had just come ashore.

Georges Kermabon who was heading back to Tahiti to finish construction of his own boat but who, at my request, stayed to give me the benefit of his experience and technical competence in working on the transmission system of the automatic pilot and in modifying the upper works of *Manureva*.

Gildas Le Guen, who, like Georges, was born in Brittany and had accompanied Georges on a tour around half the world, joined us after sailing solo from Tahiti to northern Australia. Tahiti, it seems, is the crossroads for all our friends who can't stay away from the sea.

Thus, *Manureva* was able to enjoy the same devoted attention, and the same limitless time and patience, that her bizarre aluminum hull has received since the day she was launched.

Sunday, December 30.

The sea is calm and beautiful today. During the night, I left *Grand Louis* behind and also passed what I think is *Second Life*.

It seems good to be back in the open sea. There is an enchanted sunrise of purple and scarlet to celebrate the unparalleled flight of my *Manureva*—for I've sighted *Kriter* and *Great Britain II* abeam. It's obvious that we've found our stride. I've taken advantage of this glorious sunlight to indulge myself in the luxury of a nap.

This first day is a time for putting everything in order and for various contacts with the boats in the Whitbread. I will decide the proper time for these radio breaks every day after receiving the weather report from Sydney.

There is good news: *Sayula* is sighted abeam. And there is bad news: my generator started up willingly enough, and then sputtered out and refused any further collaboration. Adding insult to injury, it is now giving off a nauseating and pervasive stench of fuel.

127

Problem with the automatic pilot at midnight. I've had to tie down the cap because the pin has come out. I've decided to sail off the wind and to haul down the mizzen so that I can get a good night's sleep.

Monday, December 31.

A sudden increase in wind from the south-southwest. After jibing, I had lowered the genoa. It is too soon to start giving *Manureva* a hard time.

During the afternoon I exchanged positions with *Kriter* and *Grand Louis,* followed by a long chat which ran down my batteries. I'm now using the little Honda standby unit.

I'm still having trouble with the generator, and I suspect that it has a bad contact. I've left it on while recharging the Honda, but so far there is no sign of life when I press the button.

I am already having trouble raising Sydney. I could not get hold of Jeff, and I finally had to send a telegram asking him to answer after he hears the meteorological bulletin for the Whitbread Race.

Tuesday, January 1, 1974.

I got up at 0100 to wish myself a happy New Year. After all, I am beginning the new year with a long voyage, and I could not ask for anything better. This stage will indeed be long: 16,000 miles, instead of the 14,000 between Saint-Malo and Sydney via the Cape of Good Hope. Long and also dangerous, because we will have to go down further, exchanging the "roaring forties" for the "howling fifties," passing

Cape Horn in a field of ice floes and sailing through areas which all the charts indicate are littered with icebergs. No doubt the first 7,000 miles will be the hardest. We are ready for them. Everything is in good shape and has already been tested in the Indian Ocean.

After Cape Horn, I will try to increase our speed. There are still some fantastic records to be challenged on the way home, and I will amuse myself by trying to do something about them. Until then, however, I am going to play it safe and play nursemaid to *Manureva*. The only important thing, at this stage, is to get around Cape Horn.

I made a decision at noon regarding my course. All of the participants in the race, except *Second Life,* have chosen to follow the route toward Cape Horn that passes the extreme southern tip of New Zealand. *Second Life* will go through the Cook Strait, which separates the northern and southern islands of New Zealand, and hopes to compensate for this longer route by picking up stronger southwest winds. At first, I was tempted to go with the majority around the southern tip of New Zealand, the shortest route, following an imaginary straight line between two points on the globe. Going the other way, the course remains constant but the distance is longer. However, in the first instance, although the distance is less, the course must be changed constantly to curve toward the pole following the curve of the circle. Weighing the advantages and disadvantages of both options, I chose to go through Cook Strait, with the idea that I could then put into Wellington for repairs on my generator.

Meanwhile, I am trying to repair it myself. I changed the spark plugs and succeeded in getting it started. It ran for thirty minutes and then stopped again. I then worked out a Rube Goldberg solution: I soaked a piece of fabric in gasoline, put it in the air filter's place, and set it afire, with the idea that it may simply be the warm-up system that is not working. Sure

129

enough, the generator started up, but then sputtered out again because it was overheating. It's possible that the trouble lies in the cooling system. I keep trying, replacing a fuse—but I am wasting my time and I know it.

Another problem: I am getting serious interference on my radio and I cannot pick up the weather report from Sydney. Fortunately, *Kriter* and *Grand Louis* heard me. I described my problems with the generator and asked them to pass on a telegram for me.

I still have the little Honda standby unit, but it requires too much fuel for me to continue using it.

Before midnight I was able to contact my parents to wish them a happy New Year—and also to explain my problems, which took sixteen minutes. I learned that *Pen Duick VI* has had to put into Sydney harbor because she has lost her mast again. It is more like a curse than a run of bad luck. That ends the race for *Pen Duick,* I'm afraid. Eric Tabarly will never be able to get another mast delivered to Sydney in time.

Wednesday, January 2.

The sea is calm today and I have time to work on the generator, trying various ways to get it started again and succeeding only in getting a series of violent electrical shocks. I've checked everything: the water level of the batteries, the possibility of water in the motor oil, the cylinder-head, and so forth. I've cleaned the platinum-plated screws, disassembled the solenoid, charged the batteries. Nothing works. The only thing for me to do now is wait until tomorrow night at 2300 when I have a ''consultation'' scheduled with Claude Savignat, a diesel specialist in Cannes.

I picked up a weather bulletin from Wellington, which is over 600 miles away.

Thursday, January 3.

The *Manureva* was hove to at 0600, and though the wind began to rise, there was no problem. The sea is still calm, with occasional wavelets sparkling in the sunlight. The wind from the southeast has put me in a good mood. I have time to read. In fact, I read last night until my eyes began to burn. This morning, I started in on *Mariage de Loti,* which has some beautiful passages and which I find both fascinating and moving.

At the meridian, my position is 36°40'S and 165°10'E. I know that yesterday *Kriter, Grand Louis* and *Sayula* reached 42°S.

I heard a few minutes ago that *Grand Louis* is in the lead. Bravo! The porpoises around the boat seem to share my elation at the news that a French boat is winning. But the sky obviously is Anglo-Saxon and it has turned a sulky gray, letting fall a fine and no doubt vengeful rain.

Kriter is trailing by forty miles; but *Sayula* is still a threat.

I contacted Claude "Diesel" Savignat on schedule at 2300. In ten minutes of the densest possible conversation, he unveiled all the secrets of problem generators. Clean the battery terminals. Tighten all screws and bolts of the control box. Strip an electric wire at both ends for a shunt. And so forth. I made feverish notes of everything he said.

Friday, January 4.

Another beautiful day. The sky cleared this morning and this afternoon saw a glorious trade-wind sky. As it grows later, the wind is picking up.

We are continuing on course for Cook Strait. I got my

charts in order, and then I once more attacked the generator. I thought that I'd found the reason for the breakdown in the warmup system when I discovered a loose wire leading to the solenoid; but that was obviously not the real problem, because the motor died almost as soon as I started it up. I've noticed that the oil is full of bubbles. An interesting but useless piece of information, since I do not know what it means.

I had radio contact with R.T.L., but obviously I cannot communicate with them regularly under these conditions. I did take enough time—three minutes—to tell them about the generator.

Saturday, January 5.

The wind died this morning, and *Manureva* is becalmed.

An albatross is following me. And the albatross is being followed by a dozen petrels, small gray birds from the Antarctic zone who will be my traveling companions in this area.

There is a swell from the south, and there are cirrus clouds in the sky. Something tells me that we are in for a blow.

While waiting, I have picked up where I left off with the generator, trying to follow to the letter the recommendations made by Claude. It is wasted effort. Total results: two burnt-out fuses and one more electric shock. I've checked as much as I can of the wiring, washed and cleaned the filters, etc. Nothing works. All I get is a couple of coughs from the motor, and then silence. Tonight, I will talk to Claude again and I hope to get new instructions.

We are moving ahead, but very slowly. For our first week out of Sydney, a total of 1,039 miles, for an average of 148.5 miles per day—not exactly a record performance. It is true, however, that I'm spending more time with the generator than with the sails, and that the wind has not been very good lately.

Sunday, January 6.

The wind seems very confused this morning and is making a complete circle of the compass. It necessitates constant veering about and setting a haphazard course.

After sending up the reaching jib and taking care of the sails, I settled down to eight hours of steady work on the generator. First, I went over each one of the operations that I had performed (in vain) in the past few days. Then I tried all of the "last resort" measures that Claude described to me last night. These concerned especially the fuel pump and the fuel injector. I ended up soaked with fuel—but it appears that the battle has been won. The generator is now working as it should. There were two things wrong with it: a broken wire in the electrical circuit, and a blockage in the fuel line. I think that the blockage was probably due to the poor quality of the fuel I took on in Sydney.

I spent the evening at the radio, talking first to *Kriter* who asked me to pass on several messages for them. I learned from Auckland Radio that it is impossible to raise Tahiti, and so I asked my operator to send a telegram to Teura for me, telling her that the generator was fixed and that I would try to contact her on the Mahina Radio frequencies.

I talked to Claude Savignat again and got a few last words of advice. Then I talked to my parents and passed on the messages from *Kriter*. Then, in order not to have to spend all evening at the radio, I asked them to let R.T.L. know that we could now re-establish contact.

As far as the race is concerned, *Kriter*, *Great Britain II*, and *Grand Louis* are still together at 50°, while *Sayula II* is further down, about seventy miles away.

133

Monday, January 7.

I saw a ship to starboard during the night. Its presence may mean that there is land nearby.

The big news of the day is that my generator does indeed seem to be functioning perfectly. It started up immediately. My mood, needless to say, is definitely up. I repaired the battens of the running jib and then filmed the porpoises gamboling in the water. They seem as happy as I am.

The weather is superb, the barometer is steady at 32.8, and the sounder indicates a depth of 607 feet. We are getting close; but everything is going well and there is obviously no longer any point in making a stop in New Zealand.

At nightfall, there was land to port: a remarkable cone-shaped silhouette. It is North Island. According to the legends of the Maoris, the island is a fish pulled from the water by the god Maui.

As the lights from Cape Egmont pass in the distance, the depth of the water goes from 489 feet to 303 feet. The barometer is falling, and now stands at 28 degrees. I wonder what will happen.

During the evening, I contacted R.T.L. through Saint-Lys Radio and gave details of the generator breakdown and its subsequent repair. I also gave a thorough account of my departure from Sydney, followed by news of the Whitbread. A quarter of an hour later, through the same operator at Saint-Lys—a super-efficient type—I was able to reach Teura at Tahiti. Finally!

Tuesday, January 8.

The sea is rough and the waves are quite high. In the distance, there are lights to starboard. A drilling platform? Or a brightly lighted ship?

I hauled down the mainsail, and then we jibed. I brought out the jib and ran it up, and then the mizzen with one reef in it. I think I have found precisely the proper speed. We will have to jibe again, then luff in order to go closer to shore. Then, when daylight comes, we will hoist the mainsail and let out the reef in the mizzen before entering the narrows of Cook Strait at slow speed.

Now, we are being greeted to the Pacific by squalls from every direction. A huge ocean against *Manureva* and me. We are trying to bear southward to find the wind. It's time for me to worry about sailing again.

The emerald sea dominates the somber arc of mountains lining the Strait. It is an impressive picture of tranquil power and rough beauty that I find fascinating. I feel refreshed by the sight of the enormous power of the elements.

Soon, there was cold air reminiscent of the mountains of Switzerland and the boat began to knock. Finally, the arrival once more of the albatrosses and the mollymawks confirms that we are once more in the roaring forties.

I hauled down the mizzen and went to bed. From now on, we are down to serious business.

Wednesday, January 9.

The sea is very rough, and I let us run before the wind throughout the night.

At 1000 I raised *Grand Louis* and learned a very sad piece of news: *Great Britain II* has lost one of its crewmen. With the disappearance of a man overboard from *Pen Duick III* en route to Rio from Tahiti, this is the fourth man lost to the sea.

A hailstorm in the middle of the day resulted in the loss of the aerial of the automatic pilot—the second one I've lost since Sydney. It's outrageous that someone could actually

135

manufacture and market such defective merchandise. In order to hold us steady on our course, I've hooked up the automatic pilot. But *Manureva* seems to be holding her own under reefed mainsail. It is good to know that she is.

I've been in touch with *Grand Louis,* which is running a magnificent race. André Viant, the skipper, asked me to pass on news from all the crew to their wives. I then spoke to Chay Blyth, captain of *Great Britain II,* to express my sympathy.

At midnight, just as it was supposed to be Thursday, January 10, it became Wednesday, January 9, again. We've just crossed 180° east and west, the international date line— that is to say, the opposite of Greenwich meridian. Thus, we've gained a day (or lost a day, according to one's viewpoint).

On this new January 9, I have the heartrending task of being one link in a communications chain relaying messages of sympathy and condolence to *Great Britain II.* One message was a telegram from Maureen Blyth to her husband, the captain, whose feelings can only be imagined.

I called Clamecy during the evening. My mother was alone at home and, after giving her my position, I promised to continue playing it safe. I told her that the sea was quite calm and assured her that I would follow a course on a latitude sufficiently high to avoid rough weather. It is not hard to guess how she must feel when she hears of a tragedy like that which has befallen *Great Britain.* I could not resist saying almost anything that would reassure her a bit.

Thursday, January 10.

I stayed in bed quite late this morning; until 0900, in fact. And then I had a leisurely day in the agreeable company of *Manon des Sources.* It was the end of the afternoon before I knew it, with a sunset of reds that foretells troubles to come.

I hauled down the mizzen—just in case.

Toward midnight, the mainsail was violently torn from the mast and the halyards and slides broken. To pick up the mainsail is a task that I would not wish on my worst enemy. I did it but, at the end of the operation, I was out of breath and weak as a kitten. All I can do is furl it on the deck and wait for better days.

The breaking of the halyards and slides worries me. This forty-knot wind is far from being a storm; and, moreover, I had taken two reefs in the sail. It seems to me that a mainsail should be able to stand more strain than that.

I've run up the mizzen, but we are not moving at more than three knots.

Friday, January 11.

Manureva is taking a beating this morning. We will heave to for a few hours and drift, then get under way with only the jib.

I am taking advantage of this "down time" to finish reading *L'Officier sans nom.* I've never before done so much reading at sea as I am now.

It is very rough outside and I've battened down the boat completely. Suddenly, as I was watching safely from inside my cosmonaut's bubble, I saw a gigantic wall of green water rise from nowhere. When it struck, we were tossed about like a piece of straw. My heart jumped into my throat, my knees felt weak, and a shout escaped my lips: "My God!" It was half-exclamation, half-prayer.

Between waves, heaven sometimes seems very close. An instinctive prayer rises and is articulated as a cry which serves to soothe and reassure, particularly in those circumstances when there is nothing left to do but turn to the only being who

137

can control the elements. Our most beautiful prayers are born at sea, not only because at sea we are like lost children asking for protection, but because, when an incredible night offers us the beauties of the heavens, when a simple and yet grandiose sunset displays its splendor for us, and when nature's most spectacular displays are paraded for our benefit alone, our hearts rise, almost in spite of ourselves, in a hymn of praise and gratitude.

In my second week out of Sydney, I covered only 1,119 nautical miles, for an average of 154 miles a day. Surely I can do better than that.

A quick look back at the past two weeks for a satisfactory explanation: it is true that, entering the Tasman Sea, *Manureva* was doing eighteen knots. It is also true that the wind was strong, but not too strong; and that life was beautiful. Yet problems came up to send everything awry: changes in course and in sail, daily struggles with the generator; navigational problems; and, finally, winds that die down and leave us in the middle of nowhere. What I need is more or less normal conditions and the chance to make up for the past few days. I feel a certain tension in my guts; and I have a feeling that it won't go away until I've rounded Cape Horn.

Saturday, January 12.

This has not been a good day. It was a day of fog and of various troubles. I was busy the whole time, doing chores here and there and trying to figure out why I had not heard anything about the race. (It was several hours before I discovered that the radio antenna was broken.) And then my generator is on the blink again—which means more hours of work: looking, screwing and unscrewing, unbolting and bolting, and, of course, burning out fuses.

Finally, I hauled down the mizzen and the reaching jib and ran up only the running jib. We are navigating on automatic pilot.

Sunday, January 13.

It seems that I'm in for a new round with the generator. I noticed that there were water and bubbles in the motor oil, and I have drained the motor. But how did the water get there?

I've rigged up a new aerial—the third one—for the automatic pilot.

Since the sea is still rough, I am using only the light genoa. I am going to run up the mizzen—reefed, of course.

Fortunately, I've been able to contact Claude, who suggested a new series of operations on the generator. First, I must check the valves and determine the rate of exhaust. Claude was as worried as I over the water in the motor and he suggested that I seal the ventilators shut whenever they are not actually in use. This means that I must set to work once more to make wooden covers for them.

Grand Louis is now at 57°S and today encountered her first iceberg. The temperature on the bridge is 34°F. *Grand Louis* is moving at eight knots despite a contrary wind, and she is 2,400 miles from Cape Horn.

Icebergs are the nightmare of my solitude. If I venture too close to the ice zone, I will have to stay awake twenty-four hours a day, a problem that does not occur when there is a crew of several men to divide the day into watches. The ice zone, of course, varies according to the time of year and the longitude. Toward the 120° meridian, it goes up to 47°S, while at Cape Horn it is at 57°. In any event, in such areas, where it is often foggy, these detached mountains of ice, floating northward for considerable distances before melting, are a constant hazard to all vessels. Some of them are indeed the size of mountains, although the one sighted by *Grand Louis* was relatively small: 100 feet high and about 335 feet wide. But if I strike even a small one, then it is good-bye Cape Horn.

I confess that I would like to see an iceberg to admire its magnificent glacial colors running through all the whites and blues and into the grays. On this trip, however, I will gladly forego that pleasure. Yet, willy nilly, there will come a time, at the moment of passing Cape Horn, when I will have to venture to within sixty-five miles of the ice. Navigation is particularly difficult there at this time of year, because it is summer in the southern hemisphere—which means that the icebergs have already separated from the mother-ice and begun their ominous journey.

For the moment, therefore, I'm staying farther north than most of the boats in the Whitbread. My route is longer than theirs, but safer.

Since I left Sydney, my feelings about the first stage have changed considerably. There were times in the Indian Ocean when it occurred to me that I might be about to die and that I was leaving nothing behind except perhaps a few memories. By nothing, I mean no one. When the final tallies are drawn up on a person's life, records have very little weight. The ocean, yawning like a black pit into which a sailor can disappear forever, makes me think for the first time of leaving something of myself which, if I should die, would continue to live after me. Therefore, while in Sydney, I discussed with Teura the possibility of having a child. The prospect is a frightening one; but Teura and I will do as well as we can.

Now I know, as I approach Cape Horn, that I am no longer alone in the same way. I have another boat to captain—a boat carrying all those that I have "tamed," as the fox says in *The Little Prince*. To tame means, in a sense, to create bonds. And my own bonds now bind me to a bit more prudence than perhaps I've shown in the past. There are times when I have to know where not to go; because I now have an obligation to return home. It is a bit like having respect for one's own existence; but it is much more like accepting the responsibility for one's affections. We are responsible for the feelings that others have for us.

That is why I would like to weight luck in my favor as much as I can: for the sake of the ones who, in a sense, are sailing with me. Now, I always buckle on my safety harness—grudgingly, perhaps, because it takes time and also because it's not very comfortable. I am no longer alone, and as I move toward the Cape my steps are more careful. Which is not to say that I have any intention of dragging it out. There is a difference between taking your foot off the accelerator and applying the brake—a margin of which I must become aware.

Monday, January 14.

I am continuing to work on the generator, checking everything, removing and then replacing every part.

Grand Louis and *Kriter,* at 57°S, are now sailing in the ice zone, surrounded by floes and even by icebergs in a temperature of 32°F. *33 Export* put out from Sydney only a few days ago and has asked me to ask *Grand Louis* and *Kriter* for their working frequencies, the times and days for radio contact, and their positions.

In the eighteen days since we left Sydney, I have become a sort of weatherman for the boats in the Whitbread. Every day, I give the boats a very complete report on the Pacific—winds, fronts, etc. I'm able to do so because I'm lucky enough to have a decoder for meteorological charts, a really extraordinary security tool. It is a kind of teletype which prints isobars, fronts, high and low pressure areas, ice charts and wave heights, analyses and seventy-two-hour forecasts. It would be an extremely useful instrument for the Whitbread boats to have, except that the rules of the race prohibit it. During the 1972 Transatlantic, since I was aware that I was neither Tarzan nor Superman, I arranged to have this unit aboard, with the thought that it would be very useful in helping me choose my route and select my sail. After the race, I was imprudent enough to admit that it had indeed been of some help, whereupon the English adopted a regulation forbidding its use. And the 1976 Transatlantic was run without the participants being allowed to decode the meteorological charts.

I have every intention of respecting this regulation; but, as I have already stated and written, the regulation, in my opinion, is arbitrary and meaningless. Why not forbid the use of the chronometer and bring back the hourglass? Surely it is not a superfluous precaution to find out where there is a storm that may sink your boat. Even with that knowledge, it is up to the sailor to know how to handle his boat in the storm. It is true that the cost of this equipment is high, and also that many boats do not have adequate room for it. But the fact remains that security should be the prime consideration in such matters.

Tuesday, January 15.

Good weather has returned and, during the afternoon, I ran up the gennikers. After hauling down the mizzen, I engaged in a rather precarious bit of gymnastics, hanging from the starboard pontoon to recover the spinnaker sheet—an operation that delayed lunch until 1700.

I had a six-minute contact with R.T.L. through Saint-Lys

Radio, long enough to submit a report: the accident with the mainsail, the hours spent lying to, the water in the generator, the loss of the antenna, and the position of *Grand Louis* and *Kriter* in the ice—and now *Adventure* has just joined them.

Wednesday, January 16.

A beautiful starlit night. Then at 0300, just as the wind was slacking a bit, the halyard of the port genniker snapped. This, of course, entailed a series of problems. First, I had to recover the sail and get back on course. Then I ran up the mizzen and had to brace about to get underway again. Finally, there were the jib booms to haul aboard . . .

The meridian has our position as 48°30'S and 149°20'W. I am one day behind *Second Life,* but four behind *Kriter, Grand Louis,* and *Sayula II.* I'm going to have to work if I want to get around the Horn before the end of the month.

To test my good resolutions, I decided to take a certain amount of trouble with my lunch. Lately, I've sort of drifted into pot-luck lunches, eating pretty much anything that I lay my hands on.

Nightfall found me in a meditative, lyric mood. "How huge the ocean is," I wrote in my log. "It is night, and my running lights are on—for my own sake more than anything else. It is a ridiculously insignificant spot of brightness atop the mainmast, tracing arabesques on the dark expanses of the immense sea. It is only a pinpoint of light; but is a symbol of life and faith. In the middle of the sea, there is a light dancing above the waves, dancing and lightening the way for a solitary sailor."

I am like a child tonight, and the sea enfolds me. I think it is time for me to go to bed.

143

Thursday, January 17.

Rough seas, fog, drizzle—but high morale aboard because I am going to talk to Teura today.

At 0600 the halyards broke for the third time in less than three weeks—very high breakage. But such things seem unimportant when I'm waiting to talk to the other half of myself.

I began trying to raise Mahina Radio at 1100 and, in passing, caught the weather report from Canberra. But nothing from Mahina. Nothing, in fact, for several hours. It was not until 1700, and through Saint-Lys Radio, that I was able to pick up a few words from my friend, relayed from Honolulu. I was so pleased that I've arranged for another contact tomorrow at noon, hoping for clearer reception.

I crossed 50°S at noon today, and we are now at the extreme limit of the ice area. I must keep my eyes open.

To celebrate my somewhat frustrating contact with Teura, I had a dish of boiled potatoes, "the caviar of the open sea." It also helped me forget about the fog and drizzle. The barometer seems to be in free fall. What next?

This evening I had a kind of round-table chat with *Kriter* and *Grand Louis. Tauranga* joined in and reported that she is also beginning to encounter icebergs. Together, we tried to figure out what kind of weather lies ahead.

Shortly before midnight, the wind shifted violently to the southwest at a speed of between forty and fifty knots, breaking the clew of the genoa as though the grommet were made of glass instead of steel. I managed to get the genoa under control and to send up the running jib; but *Manureva* took a few more nasty turns before a thoroughly drenched and chastened Colas prudently hauled down the mizzen.

Friday, January 18.

The sea was so rough and we were rolling so violently that I was obliged to let *Manureva* run before the wind. Even so, the crosswinds were very dangerous and, since I now have a new problem with the automatic pilot, I had to stay on watch under the bubble. I've lost the line of the pilot and, because of the impact of the waves, the instrument is out of kilter. Probably the screws loosened and caused the aerial to jam the pilot so that we tended to swing into the wind. I secured the pilot as best I could, as I had done off the Cape of Good Hope in 1972. I also rigged up some halyards between the bubble and the tiller—regretting all the while that I can't use the wheel because it needs repairs that I haven't yet had time to do.

There are now gusts of sixty knots and it is absolutely essential that *Manureva*'s stern be kept into the gigantic waves that occasionally manage to hit us broadside with a deafening roar.

The meridian has my position at 49°50'S. *Grand Louis, Kriter,* and *CS e RB* are at 60°S. The other boats are not much farther north.

The barometer now stands at 29. I've never seen it that low before.

We are heeling at a frightening angle and I feel absolutely helpless under my bubble. Nonetheless, I do what I can to keep *Manureva*'s stern to the waves. I've had to haul down the jib two or three times to close the hanks that somehow came open on their own. Our heel has suddenly gone from frightening to terrifying under the impact of an incredible wall of water that struck us from the south-southwest.

I feel the same kind of deep-down anxiety that I did in the Indian Ocean, and I've decided to run up the storm-jib, then jibe and head northeast. Fortunately, I was able to raise *Kriter* and *Grand Louis,* which was a boost to my morale.

145

It has been quite a day, and I will not soon forget it.

This week's figures are better: 1,367 miles from meridian to meridian which, with a total of 3,525 miles, raises my average to 168 miles per day. Just a bit more effort . . .

Saturday, January 19.

At two o'clock in the morning, completely exhausted, I took advantage of a calming trend to get to bed. I wore new pajamas—and I took a hot water bottle with me, just to keep in touch with the good things in life. Despite the sea, which was still quite rough, I slept the sleep of the just until 1100.

My schedule, obviously, is all awry, and I did not have lunch until 1800.

I think that I am about 2,600 miles from Cape Horn. No doubt, I am too far north, following the depressions. Even so, I prefer to be a selective masochist with respect to my special northern route. It seems to me that I am better off being tossed around by the wind—as long as it doesn't get out of hand— than staying on watch twenty-four hours a day because of icebergs. I've made a definite choice between option-wind and option-iceberg.

I called my family to relax a bit after my exhausting bout with the weather, but I was able to give them only an approximate position: 49°S and 134°W. I've been navigating by estimate for the past three days, since the sextant is totally useless and is resting undisturbed in its box, waiting for an improvement in the weather.

Sunday, January 20.

Thank God it's Sunday. I like to take a holiday on Sundays, the sea permitting. Today, the weather is cloudy and I spent part of my time bailing. I did, however, take a break for tea accompanied by British cookies.

Later, I finished untangling the mainsail halyard and then climbed the mast to rig a new halyard. Climbing the mast is not the chore that it was before reaching Sydney since, while in port, I had steps welded on to it. Nonetheless, once I was up there, it was long, hard work and my arm was numb by the time I finished. I was back on deck before I realized that there was no lead weight to bring the halyard down, so it was stuck midway. I had to start all over again—after a short rest—and this time I used a heavier weight than usual. Unfortunately, this problem means that there are a number of steel cables swinging loose overhead, between the rigged halyard and the spinnaker pulley which is hanging loose. From now on, I'll have to wear a hard hat when working at the foot of the mast.

At midnight, I let us go with the wind a bit.

Monday, January 21.

Dawn was purple this morning, there was no wind, and the barometer is falling. The cirrus and stratus clouds are tinged with pink. The South seems to be catching its breath for a really hard blow.

I let us run in order to set the heavy genoa and, suddenly, at 1900, there was a misadventure which could have turned into a tragedy: the pulley-frame of the main stay broke off, and it was a miracle that we did not lose the mast. While I had refitted the masts and the rigging before leaving, so that I had a very solid system that could resist almost any amount of stress, I had not paid as much attention to the shoring of the masts. Now, it was the stainless-steel plate which secures the forward shoring of the mast to the deck that had just broken like a piece of glass.

147

These stainless-steel plates are the only parts of the rigging that I did not replace; and they have therefore been with the boat since it was built. It is truly a miracle that I did not lose a mast. In fact, it is the only instance I know of where the anchoring of the main stay gave way and the mast remained intact.

Fortunately, it is an extremely sturdy mast and the rigging is eminently seaworthy; for, at that moment, everything was supported by the natural rigidity of the mast and its lateral shrouds.

To effect repairs, I used the pulley-frame from the lower mizzen stays—after using the sharp end of a pickaxe to drill a hole. The temperature was hovering between 34°F and 36°F, the wind was blowing in great gusts, the waves were breaking over the deck; after two hours of work, I was certain that I would never again be able to lift my arm.

I had the heat running full blast, of course—which brings me to another problem: once more I am having trouble with the generator. It is becoming more and more difficult to start it up.

We are now under way again, using our number one jib and running before the wind.

It is, of course, impossible to get a reading on my position because of all this fog and drizzle. I'm getting a bit tired of an invisible sun and of having to estimate a position which, by now, goes somewhat beyond "approximate." All I need now is to sight an iceberg across my bow.

Apparently, I am between the devil and the deep blue sea, so to speak. On one side is a low-pressure area that is creating a very unpleasant swell. On the other, a weather front from a low-pressure area to the south. And, as the barometer is still falling, I am being very careful and limiting my sail area.

Late in the evening, despite my experience this morning, I decided to run up the heavy genoa—just like the horseman who is thrown and feels he must climb right back on the horse. There were problems with the slides pinching the stay, because the rawhide lashings have stretched. When I have time, I'm going to have to redo the whole thing with regular rigging line, which is still the best thing.

To cap the whole thing, the bottom of my oilskins suddenly decided to dump as much icy water as possible into my boots.

It has been a somewhat less than perfect day. But then it is all of a pattern with the past few days as a whole. First of all, there were those gigantic waves—at least forty feet high—that made it necessary for me to stay at the helm for fifteen hours without a break. So, for the first time I broke out a little storm-jib that I had never used before and entrusted *Manureva* to this handkerchief-sized sail and to the automatic pilot. I should add that, at that point, the wind had fallen from sixty to forty knots; but it took a long while for the sea to calm down a bit. I am quite proud that *Manureva* got through the whole thing so well; and just as proud that I knew, almost instinctively, how the old Cape Horn sailors handled the waves—always keeping the stern into them and never, under any circumstances, letting one of them catch the boat broadside.

Obviously, tomorrow is going to be a day devoted to chores and repairs.

Tuesday, January 22.

At these latitudes, dawn is very early, around 0230. Night, which is really a sort of bright dusk, lasts only four hours or so.

I awoke to gusts of fifty knots, so I brought down the mizzen and stayed on watch until 0600. It was still cloudy, but, little by little, the sun finally condescended to peek out and

149

I was able to get a reading of sorts. I am at 53°S and 122°30′W, about 1,800 miles off Cape Horn. I wonder if I will make it by the end of the month. In any case, we are under way, using the heavy genoa and not paying too much attention to our exact course. The chart table is being studiously ignored, and I am doing some reading.

I am becoming increasingly concerned about the groaning sounds from the steering mechanism when the automatic pilot is working. They seem to be getting worse. I am going to have to try to find out what is wrong.

I had very clear contact with R.T.L. via Saint-Lys Radio, and I told of the latest misadventure that deprived me of the mainsail. I learned that Teura had telephoned and left a message for me to try to call her in Tahiti on frequency 2181. A sweet, if somewhat belated, consolation.

Wednesday, January 23.

Things have gone from bad to worse. The generator absolutely refuses to start. And I opened a new jerry-can of water to find that it has been polluted by seawater.

I wasted half a day tinkering with the generator, fiddling with the various circuits, filters, plugs, injectors. At the end of the day, I finally managed to get it started, after eight or ten unsuccessful attempts.

The sun set this evening in a bed of ominous black and purple clouds, followed shortly by a hailstorm, which played a magnificent solo on the resonant metal hull.

I had a remarkably clear connection with my family in France at midnight and brought them up to date on my progress, my problems, my hopes. I also asked them to pass on this information to *Tintin*. I have by no means forgotten my commitments to that magazine; but I can't get in touch with them directly because of the necessity for using my batteries as little as possible.

Great Britain II should round Cape Horn today. According to *Endurance,* the escort ship provided by the Royal Navy for the race, the weather at the Horn is all that could be hoped for.

Cape Horn is very much on my own mind. Since the wind put my mainsail out of commission and snapped a halyard, the weather has been so bad in these parts that I haven't been able to repair the damage. I've been up the mast, but I was not able to stay up long enough to rig the halyard properly.

For the past twelve days, it seems I've spent all my time running between the deck and the tool chest. I have only one thing in mind: to round the Cape as far from shore as possible and to get away as fast as possible. I've really had my fill of high-latitude winds.

I've changed my routine aboard *Manureva.* I am now staying on watch all night and sleeping a few hours during the forenoon.

When I get right down to it, I suppose I should not complain too much about my situation. After all, even the story of the mainmast ended happily, at least to the extent that the mast is still standing. Being at sea has accustomed me to expect anything and to be willing to bear anything. Troubles and problems run off my back like water off a ship's hull.

Thursday, January 24.

There is a leak over the chart table which, given its location, is particularly bad. It must come from one of the cabin portholes and run along the aluminum inner-planking. This close to the Cape, a leaky boat is all I need.

I am still giving the weather reports to the Whitbread boats every day after I get the news of the race. They, in turn, tell me where the ice is located.

151

A new problem, the anemometer is swinging from the line atop the mast. Possibly a bird hit it. In any event, I'm going to have to shinny up there and repair it. Meanwhile, I've rigged up a clew for the genoa. If we continue to make our seven or eight knots until tomorrow, I may be able to save the anemometer and, at the same time, get a decent night's sleep for a change.

The radio is chattering away like a flock of hens. The noise does not make navigation any easier. But I can imagine how I would feel if it were all in Japanese.

At midnight, despite all my good intentions, I ran up the light jib.

Friday, January 25.

The wind is good and we are sailing with the wind on the quarter. I took a nap at 0600. I am trying to rest as much as possible for the encounter with the Cape.

Once more, the generator is on the blink. I started it up and it ran for eight whole minutes, with much clanking and grinding, before petering out. I've gone over all the lines and circuits—cooling, fuel, electric—but it refuses to start again. I've noticed puffs of exhaust fumes at the air-intake of the warmup motor, but I don't know enough about it to draw any conclusions.

The barometer has been plummeting all day and it now stands at 29.4 degrees. Yet, at sunset, the sky seemed to be clearing and, for a while, the depressing grays were enlivened by bright reds and golds.

The tally for the week is not too bad. We've covered 1,400 miles, exactly, for a total of 4,925 and an average daily distance of 175.8.

Kriter is now only 200 miles from Cape Horn.

The launching of *Manureva* at Lorient. (Photo Gérard Monceau)

Cape Horn during a lull. Winds at the Cape reach storm velocity 300 days a year. (Photo A. Colas-Sygma)

An enormous wave, water everywhere; but *Manureva* remained upright. (Photo A. Colas-Sygma)

The solitary sailor. (Photo Sygma)

Closehauled in a tradewind from the northeast, *Manureva* zips along at full speed. (Photo A. Colas-Sygma)

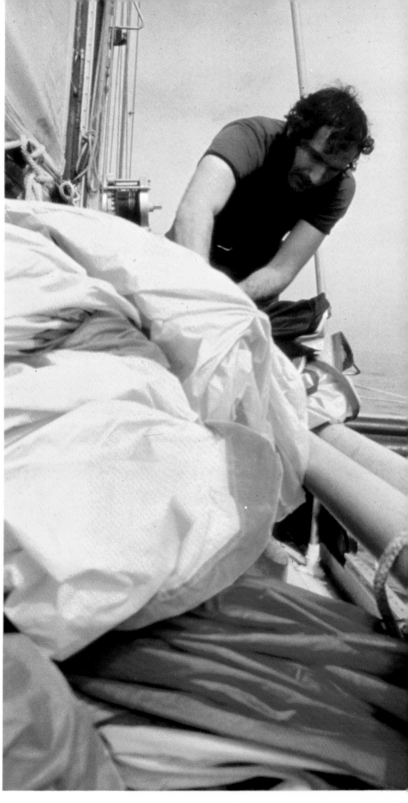

A man sailing alone spends the time shuffling the sails and maneuvering. (Photo *Paris Match*-Deutsch)

I viewed the final hours of the voyage with mixed emotions. I was happy to be home again, but somewhat sad that a page in my life had been turned once and for all. (Photo A. Dejean-Sygma)

On my way in, I had an escort of trawlers from neighboring ports and a cutter from the Bureau of Maritime Affairs. (Photo A. Dejean-Sygma)

Saturday, January 26.

Last night was gorgeous and the sky was littered with stars. The Southern Cross hung above the rigging like a candelabrum.

This morning, the weather was equally good and I was able to continue my struggle with the mainsail to get the battens and slides back into working order. I've also been able to establish my position: 54°S, 101°E.

The temperature inside is between 39°F and 50°F. I prefer not to use the heater, both to save fuel and to prevent too much contrast between outside and inside temperatures.

I spent the afternoon working on the mainsail and up the mast trying to rig the halyard. Somehow, the pulley hit me on the nose again.

I activated the little Honda emergency generator. This will be the last time, because I'm just about out of fuel.

The weather is uncertain once more, and the wind occasionally dies down completely. I then must luff so that the automatic pilot will function.

The Honda is now definitely out.

Today, *Endurance* is escorting *Kriter,* after having already provided the same service for *Great Britain II* and *Sayula II.* The two latter boats preceded *Kriter* by only three hours. *Adventure* and *Grand Louis* will round the Cape tomorrow. There is also an Italian, Ambrogio Foggar (in *Surprise*), who is rounding the Cape solo.

Sunday, January 27.

Another hailstorm during the night reminded me that the weather is not to be trusted. Nonetheless, the sea is beautiful and there is a light wind. After jibing and adjusting the din-

153

ghy, I went to sleep at 0500. I awoke at 1100 and found the sails aback. I have no idea how long they had been that way. It seems that the closer I get to the Cape, the longer I sleep. Is it because of fatigue, or am I using sleep as an escape?

During the afternoon, I rigged a wire halyard through the lift pulls and—finally!!—got the mainsail aloft with two reefs. It took me four hours to do it. One works slowly in the cold.

And it is really cold. The water temperature must be about 39°F. As far as the exterior temperature is concerned, the thermometer is not altogether reliable because of the wind-chill factor, and also because I am usually soaked when I'm topside and it seems much colder than it really is. Fortunately, I knew beforehand about this problem and I was able to give some thought to how best to protect myself. I am trying to use the heater as little as possible in the cabin, because I don't want too much difference between the temperature inside and the temperature outside. Otherwise, the transition would be too difficult. It seems that I am going in and out every few minutes. The inside temperature is therefore about 46°F. I'm delighted that I'm used to the cold. With the generator on the blink, I'd really be miserable if I had to be warm in order to be comfortable. My only source of heat is now my fire-brick, which I heat over the fire. I am very pleased with it. Of course, I dress warmly, using several layers of clothing and, on the whole, I can't complain.

Another anti-cold factor: my beard. In tropical waters I could never go for more than five days without shaving. Here, however, I have let my beard grow and it at least makes me feel warmer. It also serves as a scarf to keep the wind from getting under the hood of my oilskins (I did have an absorbent muffler, which froze the first time it got soaked.) Just about every oilskin that I've ever seen has the same defect: it lets water get in between the hood and the jacket. I hope to be able to do something about this when I get back.

Be that as it may, I do have some very sophisticated clothing to protect me from the cold. My friends at Equinoxe make sailing gear and, since they do a lot of sailing themselves, they've asked me to work with them on a material that would make life easier for sailors. And since I was going to cross some very difficult areas—the howling fifties, for example—they provided me with a double set of thermal clothing: a wardrobe that is both traditional and experimental. I am making voluminous notes on my reactions.

I had also given a good deal of thought to the problem of humidity and condensation, which so often gave me trouble. Teura found a fabric in Paris with a lining that served as padding and an exterior side impervious to humidity. The condensation, therefore, ran forward into the storage compartment used for sails—which was always damp in any case.

I also use waterproof sleeping bags. However, even when I am going to sleep only for a couple of hours (as I usually do), I want to get as much rest as I possibly can. For that reason, I try to make the conditions for sleep ideal. I put on pajamas and I use sheets and blankets. The idea is to duplicate normal sleeping conditions as much as can be done in the circumstances. There are times, of course, when I have to forego these little luxuries and fall into bed fully clothed. It also happens that I don't have time really to sleep; only to stretch out for a few minutes of rest. I then use special covers one side of which is waterproof, so that I can lie down, even wearing my oilskins, without soaking the whole bed. When the sea is too rough for sleeping in a conventional berth, I rig up a kind of cocoon in the berth. It consists of panels of cloth sewn to the side of the chest. Two steel tubes are threaded through the ends of these panels and attached to the ceiling. The whole thing resembles a sheath, and it is impossible for me then to be thrown out of bed. The only way to open the cocoon is from inside, by unfastening a series of clasps.

Any consideration of the comforts of home must, obviously, include some mention of food. I do not hesitate for a minute to admit that meals play a very important part in my scheme of things and have much to do with my morale while I am sailing solo. I have already described what I did before leaving Saint-Malo in order to make *Manureva*'s living quarters comfortable. After all, the machinery of the human body requires the same kind of care as any delicate motor, every part of which must be maintained if the motor as a whole is to function properly. The stomach is a very important part indeed of the body, and it cannot be neglected without detriment to morale and mood.

It goes without saying that I made absolutely certain to lay in ample stores of food and water. Even while keeping in mind the objectives that I set for myself as far as speed was concerned, I chose to increase the weight of *Manureva* rather than have to worry about having enough food and especially fresh water aboard. I was determined to have a two months' supply of both, so that even if *Manureva* lost both her masts and was transformed into nothing more than a triple pontoon, or even if she capsized, I would have enough food and water on hand to be able to wait, with peace of mind, to drift to shore, or for a freighter to show up. I also always have a supply of grapefruits, lemons, onions, and a large reserve of water, of which I use approximately two and a half liters a day.

In addition to the fresh food that I took aboard at Saint-Malo and again at Sydney, my friend Roger, who has a restaurant at Saint-Germain-des-Prés, and my mother with Teura's help, prepared various dishes which they then put up in glass jars. These dishes are almost enough by themselves to last two months at sea. And they certainly help to keep my insides in working order. I am not about to forget that November day in the Indian Ocean when my mother's *pigeon aux champignons* gave my morale the boost so sorely needed at that time.

The most important consideration, I think, is the absolute relaxation that I get from spending time in my little galley, preparing meals for myself. I have two more or less sacred corners inside *Manureva*. The first is the chart table, which is a large desk with a revolving chair. When I sit there, I am surrounded by familiar objects brought aboard both for their usefulness and for their decorative value: photographs, mementoes, knickknacks of various kinds, many of them from Tahiti. The second spot is my galley, with its sink, racks, and gas stove, all of which I can reach from a stool attached to the port berth (which also serves as a pantry). Fresh water comes from a jerry-can, and I can pump it directly into the sink by using a pedal at the base of the stool. Salt water can also be pumped into the sink in the same way.

There are times when I feel a need, not for any kind of prepared food that I have only to heat, but for something that I can spend time fixing myself: a special sauce, an onion fricassee—anything I feel like. The idea is not only to have a special treat, but to relax. So much so that it is usually when I am worried about the wind, or when it seems that the waves are about to get the better of *Manureva*, rather than when I have a bit of leisure time on my hands, that I get busy in the galley. At such times, I make an effort to steal time away from the helm in order to relax so that I will be rested in both mind and body if a real crisis should arise. I have the feeling—and sometimes it is a very strong feeling—that something inside me lets me know when I absolutely must relax; just as I occasionally have the feeling that *Manureva* is telling me that she needs a few minutes of rest to catch her breath, or that she feels like going at full speed for a while. It may sound ridiculous, but I really believe that captain and boat must be tuned to each other if they are going to make a go of

157

it together, and that this mutual understanding is based both on habit and on an intuition that is impossible to explain.

Finally, let me rise a bit above all this talk of food to say a few words about the culinary philosophy of the solo sailor. It should be obvious by now that I enjoy food. My enjoyment, however, is not only because of the pleasant sensation that one experiences directly while eating. It is also because, for someone alone, the preparation of good food affords a moment of intense communion with others. At that moment, it is as though I am with my friends and my family. In my mind's eye, I see my mother or Teura doing things for me, choosing this or that food, preparing something they know I like in order to communicate to me, when I open the can or the jar, their love. At such moments, I am no longer alone on the sea. One thought leads to another, and a whole series of memories goes through my mind so that I am in touch with my loved ones via the road that leads from the kitchen to the affections.

If it is true that the heart is warmed by the heat of recollected love, it is also true that, after working topside, when I go below soaked and chilled to the bone, it is an indescribable comfort for me to be in a warm, dry place. The gas fire is on—sometimes my fire-brick is on the flames—and something good is simmering on the stove alongside the brick. The atmosphere is conducive to pleasant associations and good memories, which is why I thought it important to describe in some detail how much good it does to the solitary mariner.

In any event, during the trip from Saint-Malo to Sydney I lost very little weight. No matter how rough the sea was, I always made an effort to prepare real meals for myself. When that was impossible, I had to settle for heating a casserole, which I would eat while wearing my oilskins, just in case a sudden pitch or roll sent the whole thing into my lap. Frankly, if the time had come when I was reduced to a ration of dried salami or canned goods, I don't know if I would have had the moral strength to bear it.

Monday, January 28.

The automatic pilot is not working, and, two or three times during the night, the sails were aback.

Fortunately, the weather is ideal, and I can work at repairs. I began with the pilot problem and this, of course, eventually required climbing the mast for the umpteenth time. That was no problem because of the steps that I had installed in Sydney, and because the swell has died down considerably. Nonetheless, I was a bit worried by the sight of three killer whales swimming around and around *Manureva*. These black and white mammals are quite large, sometimes reaching a length of nearly thirty feet. They can be dangerous, and these three seemed to be watching me with a look of particular impatience while I worked. With one eye on the whales, I succeeded in fastening the spinnaker pulley, then in attaching the electronic anemometer to what was left of its bracket. I suspect that the bracket was broken by an albatross. I also managed to lower the plumb-line in the mast. Then I climbed down, to find that the sail was still sticking. Up I went again.

During my radio-break for the Whitbread news, I heard that *Guia* is going to put into Port Stanley, in the Falkland Islands, for food and water; I also was able to give *Endurance* my position and explain my problem with the generator. *Adventure* and *British Soldier* have promised to help me with repairs, time permitting.

There is a soft wind and showers. If it were not for the temperature, *Manureva* could well be in the Doldrums.

With the anemometer missing its counterweight, the boat was steering between 40° and 90°, and I decided to dispense with the anemometer altogether. I've attached control lines to the tiller.

Endurance broadcasts the weather at Cape Horn every day. Yesterday, she reported unusual low-pressure areas, 28.6 degrees at 43°S and 70°W, rough seas, and squalls.

6

The hour of truth

We are now approaching our goal and it is not far ahead of us. Today's meridian establishes our location at 56°50'S, 69°30'W, while Cape Horn lies at 55°58'S, 67°38'W.

Strangely enough, just as I have come within a few days' of that point of the globe which has been at the center of my existence for so many months, I am pervaded by a kind of lassitude. The touch-and-go kind of navigation that I've had to do since leaving Sydney, added to all of the problems I've had that have prevented me from feeling that things are completely under control, has gnawed away at my enthusiasm.

The weather continues to be uncertain: trade-wind skies, beautiful weather, squalls. The shifting winds on the whole have slackened, and navigation has reflected that fact and lost something of its charm. Entries in my log have become shorter: "Tacked. Veered about. Veered about again. Squalls, cloudy weather."

Breakdown follows breakdown and repairs seem a heavy burden. In a single day, I climbed the mast five times, to grapple with the sheets, the lift, the wind indicator. I will not even mention the hours spent bailing out the bilge, decanting jerry-cans of polluted waters that have a definite smell of my fuel mixture.

I suspect that the partition in the aft storage compartment is no longer watertight. And, to top it off, the top of the automatic pilot has come loose once more, and I had to tighten the screws again while straddling the aft socle—a very dangerous perch.

The one bit of bright news was that, for the first time in many days, I managed to hoist the mainsail and it stayed up for a while. Then it began misbehaving again, breaking its slides and, finally, tumbling down so precipitously that its cap missed me only by a hair's breadth. Even my faithful foresail has had hank problems.

In these circumstances, the tally sheet for the week cannot be more than mediocre. In fact, it is quite bad: 1,090 miles for the week, which is the lowest for a long time.

Yesterday, Thursday, after the meridian I estimated that I was only 450 miles from Cape Horn, and I was able to give *Endurance* my estimated time of arrival as approximately seventy-two hours. By then, I should be at the foot of the Rock. I expect to reach the Diego Ramirez Islands, to the southwest of the Cape, on Saturday, February 2. But, when dealing with the sea, one never knows when one will arrive anywhere.

Nothing—not the sails aback in the wind, not the unintentional jibing, the dead calms, the problems with the automatic pilot, the winds shifting to the east, nor even my own foul mood—nothing now can keep us, *Manureva* and me, from moving inexorably closer, mile by mile, to the Cape, a place of storms and the site of so many tragedies.

Meanwhile, the mood of the sea is inscrutable. There is a strong swell, but no waves to speak of; and the barometer is at rock bottom.

Saturday, February 2.

I awoke to find that the wind had shifted to the northwest. I have no idea how long it has been that way.

There are clouds overhead. Toward the northeast, in the distance, I see strange white reflections—the glaciers of Tierra del Fuego?

This is certainly the day for strange visions, perhaps mirages or cloud-effects. I now think I see land at "50" on the compass. Keep your cool, Colas.

This is really the limit! The wind has now shifted to the northeast, which means that our approach to the Cape will be at a speed equal approximately to that of a turtle, tacking from west to east. That is all I needed.

The meridian confirms that we are now less than 100 miles away. We are still not coming to the wind, and the sounding apparatus still cannot give me a reading.

For months now, I have been traveling toward that mass of rocks that will soon be within sight. For months, I have been expecting storm winds to sweep me into Drake Passage, between Tierra del Fuego and Antarctica. And now, I'm here, and nervous as a racehorse on the eve of the Derby. Is it possible that I haven't done everything that I could have to make myself worthy of my encounter with the Rock? That all my grumbling in the past few days has turned the Cape against me? For Cape Horn, as every seaman knows, allows passage only to those who are worthy.

Relax, I tell myself. No one tries to round Cape Horn without knowing what he's doing and without having put himself into the proper frame of mind. And certainly, no one tries it without having taken all the precautions that, in themselves, constitute a sort of psychological preparation. A sailor does not approach the Cape without having passed through an apprenticeship of another kind, one that reaches into the very soul.

163

In the last few days, I have not been mindful of these things. But, I've been uneasy for the past month. I can't count the times that I've pictured nineteenth-century tall ships out of the North Atlantic, struggling for weeks against the current and against winds from the west. How many seamen, I wondered, had been swept overboard by those gigantic waves? How many topmast men have been catapulted from the masts by those incredible walls of water? How many worthy ships have been lost, thereby edging in black one of the most inspiring pages of human history?

I've read many accounts written by old Cape Horn men and many works of maritime history in order to immerse myself in the spirit of those men's accomplishments. I knew the fantastic story of the two ships that sailed from Holland in 1615, in search of a new commercial route to the Indies, and had the daring to sail southward along the South American coast into unexplored latitudes. There, they stubbornly entered the strait that separates Tierra del Fuego from Staten Island (Isla de los Estados) and continued on until reaching that great, dark cliff that acts as the gateway into the southern sea. The names of Shouten and Lemaire, captains of those two ships, are known and revered by every Cape Horn man. The name, Horn, in fact, is that of their home-port, Hoorn, in Holland.

Those who follow in the wake of Shouten and Lemaire do not always have the same luck as those two daring captains. Many of them never return to port. Their routes are too littered with traps, with winds too strong and ice too impenetrable. For that reason, the Cape Horn route was not greatly used at first, except for the sailing ships of the great explorers and discoverers during the Century of Light. Only gold, and the passions that it stirred, had the power to awaken courage. Then, the "Boulevard of the Pacific" came into being, leading to California and later to Australia. With increased experience and technical improvements, traffic around the Horn increased and became heavy. Magnificent sailing ships, the great clippers with their sleek lines, engaged in races against time, at fabulous speeds, on the Cape Horn route. At first, there was gold; then, nitrate from Chile. Later came new wealth: nickel from New Caledonia, lumber from Oregon, wool and wheat from Australia—all of which came through the forgotten passage first opened by Shouten and Lemaire and then virtually forgotten: that fearsome strait where the Pacific rushes into the Atlantic, where the waves circle the globe unbroken and rise from the rocks like monsters of the deep, and the winds burst out from the tunnel formed by the Andes. Out of these voyages, these formidable and permanent races in which crews battled both for prestige and for money (for, even then, speed meant profits), there arose a race of men characterized by strength and courage. In them, the spirit of self-sacrifice and patience was joined to the eternal spirit of adventure and to man's ancient love of the sea. It was a vibrant age, an age which conferred on sailing its reputation for nobility, an age which shines like a torch across time and which we must preserve in our hearts.

Legend, the child of history and time, recounts the intrepid saga of the seamen who set out to spend their lives in the Antarctic ice, sailing for Valparaiso "where others will leave their bones," as the old sailor's song has it. Sometimes it took as many as twenty voyages before a sailor was able to see the Horn in the fog, an ominous and jagged mass rising from the cold gray sea toward the dark clouds overhead. It stood there like a watchdog, bestriding the howling fifties, a tragic precipice beaten by the fury of the winds, its very appearance making it, for many, a mystic place, a Holy Grail of the sea which, though pursued, was never attained.

For mountain climbers, there are summits to be conquered such as Annapurna and Everest. For me, the Transatlantic victory was one such peak; and from there I saw the second, higher peak that I knew, come what may, I must reach. Now, in the last miles of my voyage, I stand before, not the roof of the world, but the farthest corner of the earth, Cape Horn, majestic in its forbidding solitude.

The Horn is not an enemy. It is not even an adversary in the sporting sense of the term. Rather, it is a symbol—a symbol of that which is difficult, of a certain anguish and fear to be overcome, of a great reward to be won, step by step. It represents more than an individual victory. It is part of a heritage which must be accepted and preserved. Generations of men have fought and sometimes died here. And, though we as amateurs cannot pretend to compare ourselves to them, we are privileged to continue their line. The legend of Cape Horn must be kept alive and, if no one dares any longer to confront the Cape, then it will become nothing more than a black dot in geography books. Things must be experienced, if they are to have reality. I never realized that so much as when I talked with Captain Gautier, dean of the Cape Horn men. Before sailing from Saint-Malo, I wanted to have the guidance and advice of men who had taken part in the great adventure of Cape Horn, for whom the Cape was part of their lives. I felt then how fortunate it was that the book had not yet been finally closed on the Cape, and that the experience that those men had gained from their struggles would benefit those who came after them.

I took out Captain Gautier's chart with its penciled tracings of his twenty-two roundings of Cape Horn. I smoothed out the folds and sharpened my pencil. Then, with a trembling hand, I began to draw the route of *Manureva*.

The meridian of Saturday, February 2, has us at 56°58'S and 69°24'W.

At about 1400, I sighted land. There was no doubt about it this time: islands, which my calculations confirmed were indeed the Diego Ramirez group. I have been able to get a reading from the depth sounder.

This is the first land that I have seen in almost a month. It is a strange sight, at once sinister and beautiful. I contacted *Endurance* and gave my E.T.A.: tomorrow at dawn.

Two hours later, *Endurance* came alongside. She will escort me throughout the night, and tomorrow, after rounding the Horn, she will help me with repairs once we reach a sheltered spot. Meanwhile, her crew and officers are all on deck, the officers in dress uniform on the bridge. An inspiring sight. One must be English to dine in such style at Cape Horn.

During the night, the wind dropped to nothing and I was able to get two good hours of sleep. I got up to have a look around, to stand watch in the cockpit for a while, and to marvel at the delicate geometric lines of the Southern Cross above the mainmast.

Sunday, February 3.

0300. Dawn. The sun is rising in a burst of pink and gold that covers the horizon. In the distance, I see land again; this time, the island of Hermite—and, undoubtedly, the rearing silhouette of Cape Horn, still imprecise but present nonetheless.

At the stroke of noon, I made leeway to wait for the technical team from *Endurance,* which was bringing an inflatable raft with a load of fuel, and a few supplies—and a touch of human warmth.

Here, at the edge of the world, I was going to drink a champagne toast and have some fresh bread! After weeks of solitude, lost among the towering waves, without heat or light, with no means of automatic steering since my equipment broke down, alone to face the elements, the nights on watch,

Dressed in rain suit and cap, I was ready for the weather at the Cape. (Photo Sygma)

The sunset speaks: tomorrow will be stormy. (Photo A. Colas-Sygma)

the damage, I could hardly bring myself to believe that I was going to have the undiluted pleasure of drinking a toast to my dream and to the solidarity of the human race.

Following this celebration, there were several hours of hard work on the generator. *Endurance*'s chief mechanic, with the help of two diesel mechanics, soon found the source of the trouble: the decompression solenoid in the starting circuit needed to be replaced. A screwdriver was the only tool necessary to effect this repair, and I watched closely as it was done.

The men from *Endurance* next helped me get the water out of the fuel line, and gave me fuel for the small standby generator. Then they left me alone to get underway toward the Horn which, as seamen, was the best gift they could have given me.

I approached the Cape slowly, moving in the swell toward the realization of my dream. The wind itself seemed to get into the spirit of the day by falling so as to give me enough time to feast on the spectacle before me. There was even a slight contrary breeze which served to slow *Manureva*'s progress further and prolong the feast.

It was a moment of respite before winning the prize, which would be mine in due course, for a battle won. It was a moment of tranquility in a long voyage; long in going, long in coming, and long in worry and anguish. A voyage now tarrying a moment before attaining its climax.

The pause was staged in the most beautiful weather possible; an instant of calm under azure skies, that rare phenomenon that occurs between two spells of less beneficent weather.

But Cape Horn would have been unfaithful to its own legend if there had not been something in the sky, something in the sea, something lying below the level of the senses, that had an air of menace about it. Overhead, clouds appeared and moved rapidly across the sky. Around me, the water seemed to take on a somber density as it tapped at the hull of *Manu-*

reva. A certain feeling came over me—no doubt a reflection of my own mood, tinged as it was with the memory of the seamen of old and the battles that they had waged in these difficult waters as their ships were tossed about in sudden violent squalls and they were deprived even of their sight of the Rock, the reward of all their efforts.

Today, Sunday, February 3, at the time that, in the arenas of Spain, matadors are face-to-face with their destiny in *la hora de verdad,* a boy from Clamecy is nearing Cape Horn only a few years after the sea was first revealed to him, in a rendezvous which he saw written in the sky over Newport.

Everything is going well. Our approach is slow, as is fitting for the great moments in life. I am at peace with myself. I feel somewhat lightheaded, and my respiration is perhaps a bit more rapid than usual. I can barely take my eyes from that great rock that I have so often seen in my imagination.

It is there, fragile and yet mighty, as ambivalent as all the objects of our dreams, delicate in the lacy clouds crowning its summit, solid in its massive virility among the waves. It is there, the hotly contested prize in a battle of Titans between the sea and the rock, craggy as though hewn by strokes of some unimaginable axe, furrowed by wrinkles, striped by crevasses.

The light, like the sea, is a study in contrasts. It now has a grayish hue; but is it the daylight that seems suddenly stationary between night and fog, that seems a pale shaft between two faint glimmers that are neither sky nor land? It is growing dark, and the sun is declining at the other end of the world. Its rays are reflected feebly from the ice floes, and I no longer know if the gray I see is the darkness of night or the light of day.

This meeting with my dream has given rise to such strong emotions within me that I cannot repress a feeling of profound nostalgia; for I know that it is impossible to remain immobile in time and that, for me, Cape Horn will soon belong to the

169

past. My eyes stray from the Rock to my compass, and back again to the Rock, where they linger. Then, suddenly, I have passed it. My eyes strain, and there is nothing but the mist and spray.

My wake measures the distance between the Rock and *Manureva,* and it grows steadily longer.

Manureva's wake, which so shortly before trailed into the Pacific, now measures the distance that we have come from the Rock. I think that there will never again be another experience like it. There will be nothing so enormous and weighty to move in my mind from the present to the past. Even now, memory is replacing hope within me. At the very instant of victory, what was there to remind me that all things must have an end? Is there any victory in the world that is not tainted with the gall of bitter regret?

As we continued under way, there suddenly came to me a vision of my anticipated return home to France and of the sensationalists and the professionals of doom who would assault me with their questions. I could already see their faces wreathed in professionally engaging smiles, their hands thrusting out microphones: "So, Alain, Cape Horn was a disappointment this year?" As though I had not played the game according to the rules. As though I had not followed my route around the world, from Saint-Malo to the Cape of Good Hope, Cape Leeuwin, New Zealand, the roaring forties and the howling fifties, taking my chances with the fortunes of the sea. As though unexpected good weather at Cape Horn reduced the whole thing to a charade. As though the interminable hours under sail, the unending nights on watch, the bone-penetrating cold and the frozen hands, and above all the weeks of the stabbing anxiety that were like a dagger in my guts—as though all these things were nothing. As though the lives of four men, swept overboard by the icy black water meant nothing more than that we returned to our homes with an empty place in our hearts that would never again be filled.

I rose to my feet and shouted, "No! It's not right! It should not be so!" I do not deny that every age has the right to choose its own heroes and to measure, by their own standards, the accomplishments of those heroes. But no one has the right to send a man to his death in order to get a good story. Cape Horn, after all, is not a circus act. The sea is never unfair. She alone decides, for reasons of her own, if those who respect her will go gently to their hour of truth, far from the crowds and far from the world, for an instant of happiness so rare that it has no name.

7

The last straight line

Once I've made the final turn out of Drake Passage, I'm going to have to get under way as soon as possible. Somehow I feel that, once *Manureva* is out of the inhuman latitudes, I will be able to get back into a racer's frame of mind and make some headway. I'm already behind schedule: *Cutty Sark*'s record between Sydney and Cape Horn was twenty-three days. It has taken *Manureva* thirty-eight.

But you don't enter an ocean without paying a toll. The night of February 3, the Atlantic had prepared a sort of welcoming party for me in the form of bad weather. The warning signs had been right. The following day it was still drizzling, the water was quite rough, and the temperature dropped to 37°F. I was very tempted to head north as fast as I could; but first I had to get far enough from shore and round Burwood Bank—where, if my luck did not hold, I might find a wave with *Manureva*'s name written on it.

In the middle of a squall, I saw a magnificent rainbow to the south. There were large albatrosses escorting me and, even at night, the polar halo was there, like the light of a full moon, refusing to abandon us to the darkness. The sea, even when it threatens, does not refuse favors to the sailor.

The following day it continued wet and cold. The sea was still rough and I remained at the tiller continually, watching every wave so that we would not be somersaulted stern over stem. Squall followed squall until my hands began to shrivel from the constant wetness. There is an old railroadmen's saying that one storm can give birth to another. That was exactly what was happening; and it seemed to me that the bit of folk wisdom expressed in the adage might well be applied to the sea.

The waves did not allow me a moment's rest. I did try to take advantage of a period of relative calm to stretch out on my berth for just an instant, when a particularly heart-stopping list doused the cabin and my chart table thoroughly. It took me 300 strokes with the hand pump to bail out the water. My legs were still weak and trembling with emotion while I worked.

The generator, once more, has broken down and has not worked since yesterday. For the past two days I've been using the storm jib. I haven't dared try to head north because the sea is so rough. The waves are from 35 to 50 feet high. Nonetheless, I've now made a decision: the first time that I sight a school of penguins, or the first relatively calm weather that arrives, we will go hard to port and head due north. The ice is not far away and *Manureva*, taking advantage of the storm from the west, in forty-eight hours has already covered half the distance between Cape Horn and the South Georgia Islands.

Wednesday, February 6.

Everything is going better this morning. The barometer is climbing, the sun is peeking out, and the sea is gradually becoming calmer. With the mizzen hoisted, and *Manureva* set on a northward course, I fell into bed and slept like a rock. I was utterly exhausted by the hours spent at the tiller, watching each wave as it loomed up and telling myself, "Now, Colas, veer! Everytime you veer you're one step away from Cape Horn and one step closer to home!''

Toward the end of the day, after having installed four new slides, I was finally able to hoist the mainsail.

The next few days confirmed me in my good mood. With the Falkland Islands lying 200 miles to the west-southwest, I truly had the feeling that Cape Horn was behind me and that I had reached the outer edge of the really dangerous seas.

They were calm days, but active nonetheless. I had clothes to dry, the aft compartment to bail out, the forward storage bins to organize, the electric circuits of the generator to check out (it was still not working).

The interior temperature hovered at about 64°F and I felt almost indecent without my heavy sweaters and my oilskins. Between maneuvering and climbing the mainmast to run up a mended pennon, I even found time to patch a pair of outrageously ragged pants, to observe the tea-hour every afternoon—in a word, to begin living again.

I was particularly careful with the mainsail because, even though the sky was clear, there were occasional gusts strong enough to make me worry about mishaps. Meanwhile, a little voice inside me kept whispering, ''Don't be an idiot! Get home as fast as you can!''

The tally of my sixth week out of Sydney shows that I've covered 1,288 miles. The total mileage from Sydney is 7,303, for a daily average of 173.8 miles and a speed of 7.2 knots. Alain Colas, wholesaler of miles. . . .

Sunday, February 10.

Last night, I was topside maneuvering in my pajamas. What luxury!

My meridian position is less than 600 nautical miles from Buenos Aires. I'll try to establish radio contact this evening. Just a little farther and I'll be out of the roaring forties.

Manureva has now covered half the distance of this second stage; but we're going to have to hustle if we're going to make it back to Saint-Malo before the end of March; that is, before the end of the ninety days that I set for myself.

The barometer is falling and the sunset—the whole horizon was a dirty pink—promises nothing good for tomorrow. Rather than risk running into a line of squalls, I hauled down the mainsail.

I am going to have to make a decision, in the next couple of days, concerning navigation lights. Until now, the icebergs in these waters guaranteed that any ships in this area were using their radar and would pick me up on their screens. But once I've passed the thirty-eighth parallel, there will be no more ice. At that point, I will either have to show lights or stand watch at night and take naps during the day.

Wednesday, February 13.

We've now reached the level of Montevideo (to port) and the Cape of Good Hope (to starboard). In fact, I think we're too close to Montevideo, but it was important to head north and to put as much distance as possible as quickly as we could between ourselves and those latitudes which seemed designed by nature exclusively for masochists.

The sea has been rough for the past couple of days. Occasionally, I've had to lie to; and I've been using navigation lights at night. The wind from the west and the strong swell indicate that there is bad weather somewhere. We are, in any case, now out of the forties—just barely out, but out nonetheless.

It is about 6,000 miles from here to Saint-Malo; which is to say a distance equal to twice that of the Transatlantic. The weather, though not all that bad, is eating up my meager electrical supply, because I have to make use of the Decca automatic pilot to hold our course. If this keeps up, I'm going to have to resort to manual steering and, when I can't be at the helm, to head eastward under full sail. Frankly, I've just about had it with machines that never seem to work properly. The whole trip has been one breakdown after another, and they've taken much of the pleasure out of it.

Friday, February 15.

I've had nine consecutive hours of sleep, which did a great deal to settle my nerves. Until then, I was in a very black mood indeed. I'm still having problems with the speed indicator, and it's impossible for me to use all the sail that I want. *Manureva*'s bow seems to swing every which way; and we spend a lot of time in unplanned jibing. My only consolation was that, yesterday, I saw several flying fish; and, yesterday also, at dawn, there was a magnificent double-sun effect which climaxed in a triple-sun!

Manureva has now covered 1,700 of the 3,700 nautical miles between Cape Horn and the Equator—a distance which *Cutty Sark* covered in twenty-six days. We are almost halfway there, and, so far, it has taken us eleven days. This gives me a pretty good idea of our time.

I've just noticed an interesting coincidence. The crossing of *Cutty Sark* which took the longest time is the one that corresponds most closely to the time of the year of *Manureva*'s trek. *Cutty Sark* left Sydney that year on December 14 and reached the Channel on March 16. Another departure from Sydney on January 7 ended in an arrival in the Channel on April 8.

My figures, at the end of the seventh week, show that we've covered only 1,001 miles in the past seven days. This is the lowest figure since putting out of Sydney.

Monday, February 18.

I awoke this morning to find the jib backwinding, and *Manureva* moving on a northerly course at five knots.

There are squalls today and the weather is dark and cloudy with a temperature of 75°F as we cross the Tropic of Capricorn. Yesterday, at the meridian, we were only 170 miles off Rio. With the winds that we've had, if I had headed for Rio three days ago, I would have reached the city in time for breakfast and edged out the Italian boats in the Whitbread. However, if I had my choice, I would prefer to be farther toward the east than I am. I need to make a few right turns to get more out into the open sea. Cape Frio is only 120 miles away, and the Brazilian coast is notorious for its shallows. I don't want to take a chance of running aground at this point.

Still about 5,500 miles to go. Buck up, Colas!

Thursday, February 21.

A day of relaxation for the captain of *Manureva*, who spent most of his time in leisurely reading. I am about 400 miles from the point where our course will intersect the course we followed on the first leg of our journey. There is something hypnotic about this vast watery desert which seems to stretch into infinity.

For the past few days I've been very busy. I've spent whole afternoons on the generator, testing the various circuits and lines. I still can't get it started without jumping it; and even then it refuses to hold a charge. There have been the usual chores, such as mending the jib, cleaning everything, arranging gear in the aft compartment, trimming mildewed bread, and so forth. I found two jerry-cans of water that had been polluted by seawater. The stoppers must have become loose since we left Sydney and I suppose the waves breaking over the cockpit did the rest. Fortunately, I have a reserve of water bottles in the hold and, if I shave less often, there will be no problem with fresh water.

I used the brackish water for a luxurious bath, scrubbing myself from head to toe and, as a supreme act of self-indulgence, I even changed my sheets and put on an Indian shirt to mark the occasion.

As far as radio contact is concerned, I've had practically no news of the race since rounding Cape Horn. Reception is very bad in these waters and, of course, I have to use electricity sparingly because of my useless generator. Since February 18, fortunately, Daniel Millet, skipper of *33 Export*, has been relaying messages for me. In that way, I've been able to be in touch with my parents, and also with my friend the diesel expert to explain what is happening with the generator. I've gotten some suggestions from him about how to repair what is wrong.

Friday, February 22.

A calamity: the wind has died completely. I am outraged!

For the eighth week out of Sydney: 1,304 miles, for total mileage of 9,608. My average speed has increased slightly to 7.4 knots.

I've found a break in the radio antenna, which accounts for the loss of power that I've experienced in transmitting. I've

179

used the little Honda emergency generator to recharge my batteries to contact Saint-Lys Radio this evening. I've written down a detailed description of my troubles with the generator, because I also expect to be able to contact Claude, the diesel man, tonight. Then I felt free to call my parents to let them know that I am all right. I told them about the approach to Cape Horn and the meeting with *Endurance*, and I described the actual rounding of the Cape in absolutely calm weather and the strong southwest wind the next day which carried us along for two days. I tried to omit nothing: the flooding of the cabin; the moment when I was able to turn north like a diver rising to the surface for a first gulp of life-giving air; my escape from the forties and my continuing northward course toward Rio while staying in the wake of the lead boats in the race, a course I knew to be ice-free; and, finally, once past Rio, the north winds that let me move eastward in the Atlantic.

We are now getting near the trade winds and the Brazilian current is becoming less noticeable.

Sunday, February 24.

Our position is between two markers: Trinidad to port, and the island of Martin Vaz to starboard. These, of course, were the same islands that served to mark the routes of the tall ships beyond the capes.

Believe it or not, at 1600, I managed to get the generator working again! After two days of unremitting work, I found out what was wrong. Naturally, it was something that, if only I had known, I could have repaired in a few minutes: a loose connection in the junction box between the batteries and the generator itself.

Now, sitting calmly at my transmitter, with real light, and

with my navigation lights glittering away at the top of the masts, I can call my parents without worrying and have one of those heart-to-heart talks that I've missed so much for the past month.

It seems to me, in fact, that the generator is working better than ever; no doubt because, in trying to find the trouble, every part has been cleaned and every circuit checked and re-checked. Along with the charge in the batteries, my morale has climbed and I will now be able to navigate in peace without having to stay on watch from dusk to dawn because of the lack of navigation lights. What a pleasure it is to know that I can have electricity whenever I need it. It was not just a matter of reduced radio contact. I also did not have heat, light, and navigation lights. The minimum charge that remained in the batteries had to be kept for use in case of major repairs. My only light was a flashlight, which I held under my arm or in my mouth, as circumstances required.

Thursday, February 28.

The weather has been magnificent for the past several days. The water is calm; the temperature hovers at 77°F; the air is crystal clear. The sea is like a broad highway; and, at night, Ursa Major is high in the sky, while Venus sparkles like an improbable jewel. Every day, a little rainbow of droplets of water precedes us at the bow, like a triumphal arch erected in *Manureva*'s honor.

Manureva is in excellent shape and she has already knocked a day off *Pen Duick IV*'s time between the Cape of Good Hope and the Equator on the run from Réunion to France. As expected, we have encountered the trade winds, and we have just reached the latitude of St. Helena. According to racing wisdom, this stretch of sea is "the best sailing in the world."

I am spending many tranquil hours reading accounts of life aboard the tall ships, talking to my parents, and fishing for gilthead. I talked to Teura, who is getting ready to fly from Tahiti to Paris. It makes my head spin to think of the contrast in speed between my boat and the airliner that she will take.

I was in such a good mood after talking to Teura that I pumped out the water we had taken on when I left the forward hatch open in an attempt to improve ventilation.

Friday, March 1.

Our position is 5°24'S and 28°55'W, well into the domain of the trade winds. We have a brisk little breeze, our sails are like clouds on the sea, and the skipper is getting his fill of samba music from Brazilian radio stations.

Very soon, I am going to have to decide on a route around the Azores. Do we pass them to the east or to the west? I still don't have enough weather information to be able to decide. The only solution seems to be to ask for information from Paris. The National Weather Bureau no doubt will be able to give the position of the "intertropical front" and the position and probable movement of the high pressure system in the Azores. I asked Jeff yesterday to try to get as much information as possible.

Ask and you shall receive. I've just had a call from Jeff with the information I asked for. The tropical front begins at 30°W, curving between 6°S and 3°N. The Azores high is further north than usual, with probable movement toward Ireland and the Channel within the next two weeks. It may be quite severe and the bureau is forecasting a pronounced extension toward Ireland. Consequently, there will be strong winds from the north-northeast between the Canary Islands and the coast of Spain.

I now have all the elements I need for a decision. If I go too far west of the Azores, I will run the risk of being becalmed. And if I go too far east, I'll encounter very strong head winds. The best course, therefore, seems to be to move northward, but without coming too close to the Spanish coast; at about 45°, say, make for the Channel without getting close to Cape Finisterre. I should then be able to take advantage either of winds from the north, or of the western current.

We are now 360 nautical miles from Cape San Roque. The tall ships sailing in the opposite direction along this route were wary of this spot because of the danger of being pushed off course by wind from the southeast.

I saw an enormous pink physalia alongside, just as I finished reading an account by Chay Blyth in which he mentions a similar encounter.

Luck is with me. I narrowly missed having a serious problem with the mast. One of the new stainless-steel plates, which anchor the foot of the mainmast to the deck, has sheared because of stress. I immediately hauled down the genoa, eased the mainsheet, and set up the housing for the port genniker winch, making sure to give adequate slack. Then, after climbing the mast for a thorough check, we got under way again.

This, of course, is the second time that I've had this problem—all because I thought there was no need to replace parts which, as it turned out, were worn. I've now slackened the rigging somewhat, and we are under reduced sail, at least as far as the forward rigging is concerned. Also, I am going to have to follow a more westerly course than I wished, because it will be easier on *Manureva*. I must admit that, for the past few weeks, we have been doing a lot of beating; but then the wind was not very strong.

Actually, the boat is in excellent shape now because I've had time to do proper maintenance and repairs. My genoas took a beating in the Pacific, when I used them instead of the mainsail. The light genoa, in fact, was in shreds when I hauled it down at the beginning of the storm after Cape Horn.

In the past week—the ninth—we've covered 1,129 miles, for a total of 10,734 miles since leaving Sydney. Our average speed is still slightly above seven knots. According to my calculations, with the help of "Read's Marine Distance Table," I will reach Saint-Malo in twenty-four days, if we follow a straight course and maintain our speed.

Tuesday, March 5.

On Sunday, March 3, we crossed the Equator at 28°22′W. Right now, my table shelters a charted course for France and, of course, for Clamecy. A mere hop of some 3,400 miles.

It took us twenty-eight days from Cape Horn to the Equator, while the average time of the *Cutty Sark* was twenty-six days. Given the circumstances, I have no complaints. *Manureva* has even cut three days from the time of *Pen Duick IV* during her run from Réunion to France.

We are now surrounded by ominously towering banks of black clouds. The rains are torrential. I've never seen rain quite so heavy. My hands and feet are never dry—in fact, I think I'm growing scales—and everything else aboard is soggy and damp. Nonetheless, I'm trying to reap whatever advantages I can from the weather, and I soaped myself from head to foot and then stood out in the rain to rinse off. I've also caught the rainwater to replenish my supply of water—which was not hard to do, since the rain was so dense that it was almost a compact mass.

The wind on the whole is from the northeast, and the swells sometimes rise to a height of thirteen feet. Conditions seem to get worse instead of better, and I think that we are in for some well-muscled trade winds.

My chart table is a privileged place where I work at navigation. The photographs and other familiar objects help me to feel in touch with the world. (Photo J.P. Laffont-Sygma)

Pages following: Extracts from *Manureva*'s log. (Photo Flammarion)

54e jr/ le mercredi 31 octobre 1973

HEURE	VENT	MER	CAP	LOCH	OBSERVATIONS
0300	NW!W 4 25 ds	agitée à ps	70	7287	empanné
0330					grain bg lui st beau surfs dur le joue point
0500	W-30 av	fte	130	7307	à dégager d'un empanage automatique 5 lattes assés à l'artimon des surfs avec autléis et vous de gite qui font attiger des suers
0930	W 25 ds	"	120	7352	chassé pille gueulo Je dois prendre mon jour tester coulé et aligner 9 heures de sommeil.
					Ça se calme petit déj en compagnie de Fernandel et Guillan
0045 B	W!SW-20 4	agitée	130	7364	MERIDIENNE ∅231 ∅ { φ=40°25',5 G=44°E
1145 C	pris une heure de montre démarré 6.t. démarrage diffce le 3 essai				(FRED = GMT +3h)
1400		arrêt 6t			affalé artimon établi gd voile
1419	W-SW-20 4	agitée	135	7387	OTE HTR. (Albert) borroti jn bruse
					tout l'après-midi j'ague au couchant (tirmotis) artimon, 5 lattes à changer 2 coulisseaux explose établi artimon
1800 1900	W-SW-20	"	145	7431	empanage automatique : 3 lattes bg lui sorti de l'empanage par un 360°.
2130	W-15	fte bleu "	140	7452	

solution semble être de prendre le NW bd amure,
filer la gd voile d'abord en conservant Art et gd génois, puis
reprendre à la rotation W et conserver les amures de td, quitte
faire un peu de rte Sud.

```
 3° 28' 30"
    12' 30"
 89° 60'
 53° 41'
 06° 19'
 4° 06',5 S
 0° 25',5 S .
```

* question gennachers, dans la brise, lorsous
fte tension l'émerillon du mousqueton de
drisse ne doit plus étaler, ce qui explique
l'absence d'enroulement lors des hauts et la
rupture de la drisse, alors que la torsion
à l'amure allait jusqu'à mettre la toile en huit
Essayer par brise (et brises neuves) avec les
émerillons d'origine.

```
0 S / G = 45° Z / D = 14° 08',7 S

 19' 59"    46° 59' 40"
   + 16"       + 12' 20"
 20' 15"    hv 47° 12'
   05",2    Hc 46° 33',7
   03",8     ┌─────────┐
   09'       │ I = 38,3 │
             │   + près │
             └─────────┘
   51' E


→ 46° 28' + 41' / 180
   +    5,7  / 115
             Zv = 295°
  46° 33,7
```

38   Le dimanche 3 février .. 1974

HEURE	VENT	MER	CAP	LOCH	OBSERVATIONS
					La croix du Sud est au dessus du grand mât
					un nouvel objet à filer les caméras, que la
0300	ENE 2	belle houleuse	100	7496,5 vire	l'aube . levé de le 30. Th. barosté
0530	"	"	10	7503,7	lever du soleil ds 110, dr rousset germin een.
					latitude 15-40 ? Hora 5 . sondeur 22
1140	en pêche ∅ 23 ✳	{φ = 56° 02'S G = 67° 38'W}			intervention à bord
					le l'équipe technicienne
					d'Endurance, amenée en zodiac
1200				7506,9	avec pain champagne et chaleur humaine
					Heures laborieuses sur le G.E. enfin
					les charges avec le Honda ravitaille
					40 litres d'essence
					Succès, c'était le solénoïde de
					décompression qui vient de démarrage
					qui l'ont empêché. Ah, ele vanaris pun
1600	SE 8	belle houleuse de eine	60	7519,95	passé le Horn, à un mille environ 2
1615	"	"	90		remercie l'ENDURANCE d'une brassée "OW
1645			80	Sado	260.280 - sondeur 125m
1700	" 10	"			QRX course - ENDURANCE
1900			90	Sado	eh là, mais sont précisément revenus de l'Atlant
1930	4	"	50	7525,05	dégagé l'hélice quelot, branché Decca
					solide dîner pour retrouve le big ours
2130	"	v	70	7531	(au pain frais, etc...)

COGITATIONS

Un morceau de *plomb* — rouiller les glaces et filer ?

ENDURANCE   B.F.P.O. (Ships) London   (-Cutty Sark)
                                            - Wardroom Mess

chargé aussi circuit de fuel
engagé l'eau quircuit longtemps
du tank. Obligé de couper sans à le
répette pour couper court à ces histoires là-

(penser à mettre de l'huile to le Honda)

        Cutty Sark   ⎰ 23
                        ⎱ 24
        Sydney—Cap Horn 24 ½
                         38
                         23
                         31
                         29
                         28
                         24

le mercredi 6 février · 194?

HEURE	VENT	MER	CAP	LOCH	OBSERVATIONS
0100 0130 0200	marin	efforts pour			joindre St LYS Radio
					la mer s'établique moyen
0600	W¼NW 30	agitée	70	8002	lissé l'artimon et mis CAP au NE ...
					puis au lof en se lissant
					...
					...
1142 Q	W¼NW 30	agitée	10	8036	hre Méridienne ☆ 165 ☆ { H = G =
1242 P	prenons deuxe de monter				(FRED = 6ᵐ + 3ˢ) lat₀ 990 mℓ n
1431	W¼NW 28	agitée	10	8050	grand soleil, baro en hausse tvde DTE. HTR. (observation diffⁱ le bd H à 8 h ... et les embruns
1900	"	"	15	8082	
2330	WNW 25	agitée ¼ froid	30	8113	pris 4 rouleaux cont h eureux gd vle et à ... Bordé au près bon ...

COGITATIONS

P = 54°S / G = 52°W / D = 15°34',5 S

7h 31' 25"   45° 54' 5 0"
  + 3' 20"   + 12',4
17h 34' 45"   hv 46° 07',2
  71° 28',1   Hc 45° 49',5
  + 8° 41',3
  80° 09',4   I = 17,7
  52° 09,4 W   + près
  28° →   45° 18' / +55   180
           + 31',5   +140
                     Zn 320°
  Hc 45° 49',5

T. lau = 12 h 14' 07"
G = 52°W = + 3 h 28'
           15 h 42'

Cape Horn, February 3, 1974. A letter sent by the author to his parents via *Endurance*.
(Photo Flammarion)

Despite the tropical downpours and the rotten weather, we are managing to make decent time between squalls, even though *Manureva* has a tendency to knock a good deal in the swells.

I've had to stay on watch several nights because of the proximity of the Rocks of St. Peter and St. Paul. One night, I was able to get Radio-Television Luxembourg on the radio, and it was like a touch of home as I listened to the music. I had the urge to call in and report that, although the weather at the Equator left something to be desired, we were making headway all the same.

Thursday, March 7.

This morning I picked up seventeen flying fish on deck. Dressed with a lemon and the juice of three grapefruits, they made a scrumptious meal which I enjoyed to the music of "My Fair Lady" over the B.B.C. After that, a nice nap, followed by a bit of reading. I feel in tiptop shape again.

Despite a few hours in which the swells were enormous and gray clouds promised squalls, the sea has been rather calm since yesterday. The clouds finally cracked open and the sun appeared. The northeast trade winds are not at all what one might imagine; all sunlight and good wind. On the contrary, the winds sometimes are almost gales, and the squalls are quite violent. Even so, *Manureva* forged ahead, paying as little attention as possible to these somewhat depressing circumstances.

Feeling that I deserved a treat of some kind, I had cookies with my coffee this afternoon: marvelous little cookies baked especially for me, over a wood fire, by a baker at Villiers-sur-Yonne, which is not far from Clamecy. They were still remarkably fresh; and, since no one was looking, I licked my fingers clean.

I've just calculated the average time of *Cutty Sark* on her return voyages between the Equator and the Azores: 17.7 days. Between the Azores and the Channel, it is 8.8 days. Even though I took it easy between Sydney and Cape Horn, to err on the side of safety, I've made up for it between Cape Horn and the Equator. All things considered, I wouldn't be surprised if, on the last leg of the journey, I managed to outdo *Cutty Sark* by the time I reached Saint-Malo.

Monday, March 11.

We crossed the Tropic of Cancer under a cloudless sky. The weather has been spectacular for the past several days, and the temperature has been ideal. I've been relaxing, reading, listening to music, talking to my family, and trying to keep up my average speed. It's been a while since we passed the latitude of Dakar and the Cape Verde Islands. Last Friday, the end of the tenth week, we covered 1,315 miles: a total of 12,049 nautical miles out of Sydney.

The sky at night is as gorgeous as it is during the day and I can see simultaneously the Pole Star, my old friend Cassiopeia, and a lovely little satellite flitting from constellation to constellation.

Friday, March 15.

My meridian position is 32°30′E and 31°20′W—about level with Madeira and 380 miles south of the Azores. A school of dolphins has escorted me for the last few days. We've been passing through fields of sargasso weed which brings to mind a verse of Charles Péguy:

> *Et nous arriverons dans la mer des Sargasses,*
> *Trainant notre inutile et grotesque carcasses . . .* *

Since I've had nothing to read for the last few days, and nothing even to reread, I've decided to get down to some serious work. First of all, I've begun putting my notes in order, which I find very exacting and tiring work. Then, to relax a bit and also to see what it would feel like, I took pictures while hanging from the mizzenmast as the sea dug deep valleys in the swells.

I am going to have to keep my eyes open, since we are in a very busy shipping lane. I've seen several freighters and tankers.

We've covered 1,262 nautical miles this week, for a total of 12,049 miles and a slightly increased average speed of 7.2 knots.

Monday, March 18.

We've been running into squalls since yesterday and I've had to remain on deck, wet and chilled to the bone. The temperature today dropped to 57°F. There are forty-knot gusts, the swells sometimes rising to a height of twenty feet. I've had to haul down the mainsail because of unpredictable waves from the west and northwest. I put it off as long as possible, because yesterday it took six tries before I could get it up

---

*And we'll reach the Sargasso Sea
trailing our useless, grotesque carcasses . . .

again. The halyard keeps getting tangled. I was exhausted by the end of the battle, since I had spent a (traditional) sleepless night watching for Santa Maria, the southernmost island of the Azores.

It is cold, and the dolphins and sea gulls would be wearing ear muffs if they had any. Apparently, I've been acclimatized by my trip around the world, because it bothers me hardly at all. I am warm and cozy within my tiny domain.

The squalls at least have given *Manureva* such a push that she almost equalled the time of *Cutty Sark* between the Equator and the Azores. She is only a half-day short; thirteen days for us, twelve and a half for *Cutty Sark*. Even then, *Cutty Sark*'s log implies that the watch caught a glimpse of Santa Maria in clear weather—and then only from the crow's nest. Obviously, the crow's nest of *Cutty Sark* is a bit higher than the deck of *Manureva;* and this, at least in my opinion, equalizes our positions.

We are holding steady at ten knots because of the west wind. I could go even faster if I were not so set on reaching port with everything on *Manureva* still intact. There are times when I play around with the idea, reaching speeds of from fifteen to eighteen knots. But the time came when these speeds were too much for the condition of a genoa I had rigged forward. I heard a soft cracking sound, and watched as the sail tore slowly. There was no loud explosion such as I heard at Cape Horn when we lost the light genoa.

Since then, I've been using the running jib and the mainsail, with a single, deep reef, and the mizzen, but rigged in such a way as not to put undue stress on it. I am having trouble holding back *Manureva,* because she is like a horse who knows that it is nearing home. We are now almost at the level of Madrid, about 500 miles off the Portuguese coast. I think we will probably arrive next Sunday or Monday.

Wednesday, March 20.

We are less than 600 miles off Saint-Malo, at 42°14′N and 13°W. Ouessant is 480 miles to the northeast.

I've had to haul down the mizzen because of rough seas. The waves are over twenty-five feet, and I am completely exhausted by the beating I take from the waves as I try to haul down sail and then hoist it up again to make headway. Because I am so tired, I tend to move slowly; and this means, of course, that I am wasting time. It is tough going, but I console myself with the thought that tonight I will be in the Bay of Biscay.

Despite the poor sailing conditions, I am using more sail than I should. The boat can take it, and I prefer to have it a bit rough for a while rather than to stay in one place and suffer for a longer period of time. To prevent any damage, I have been staying on watch, most of the time in the cockpit. My sleep consists of twenty-minute cat naps in the armchair at my chart table. Then I go back on watch.

We are now quite near the coast and there are many ships in these waters. I am concerned about safety. In this kind of sea, it is a question of survival rather than of courtesy; and I want to be showing every light whenever we encounter a ship. According to international regulations, sail always has the right of way; but you can't always depend on regulations. A ship has to see you before giving you the right of way; and a small boat must always be ready to cede the right of way to a larger vessel.

I would like to be able to get the right wind to take us away from the coast and from these shipping lanes so that I can relax and get some sleep. So far, however, I've had no luck in that respect.

I've begun to take vitamins to keep up my strength.

Jeff informs me that my family and friends will all be on hand to give me a big welcome; that the municipality of Saint-Malo wants to give me an official welcome at city hall; and that the television people want to carry my arrival "live." The only trouble with all those plans is that sailing vessels do not run on schedules like trains, and it is hard to commit oneself to an exact date, let alone a precise time.

Friday, March 22.

The barometer is falling, but the wind has died almost completely. I tacked eight times this morning. Yesterday, the first day of spring, my log is full of references to tacking; and the red sunset promised more tacking for today.

Today is the end of the twelfth week. I've covered 1,224 miles, for a total of 14,535 miles. The average speed is 7.2 knots.

In the past twenty-four hours, we've covered only sixty-nine miles. At this speed, we'll be at sea for another week yet!

I wanted to surprise Captain Gauthier, and I had Jeff get me his telephone number in Saint-Lunaire. The sound of his strong, warm voice was enough to console me for having to give up hope of reaching Saint-Malo on Saturday. At the moment, I am in a kind of tunnel of clouds, without a single stirring of wind, dragging along like a wounded whale off the coast of Bordeaux.

Saturday, March 23.

No wind yet, but plenty of fog. So near, and yet so far.

Manureva limps along, like a bird with a broken wing. I am trying to be patient and to smooth her feathers so that she will look her very best when we do finally reach Saint-Malo.

Tuesday, March 26.

It seems that there is no end to the sleepless nights. Traffic is heavier and heavier, and ships appear only to be swallowed up almost instantly in the fog. The depth sounder picked up the bottom yesterday, then lost it again. Where are we?

The weather report from Brest-Le Conquet keeps repeating its litany of despair: "A stationary front . . . fog at Ouessant . . . Clouds . . . Visibility zero."

The fog, in fact, is like a curtain, except in those rare instances when the sun manages to make a small tear in it.

Ouessant is still 108 miles to the northeast. We are tacking and tacking again with monotonous regularity. A short while ago, we passed a trawler in the fog. She made a half-turn and came back to see who we are. I hope she passes the word. I am going to ask Brest-Le Conquet to broadcast a message to trawlers in the waters west of Brittany, north of Gascony and the western Channel: "Warning. Twenty-four-hour watch is no longer being maintained aboard *Manureva,* a sailing vessel sixty-seven feet long moving between the Bay of Biscay and Saint-Malo." If I am going to have to stay on watch all night, obviously I am going to have to be able to rest during the day, at least as long as I am not too near the coast.

In six days, I've covered only two days' normal distance. I don't have time even to take off my clothes, and this will be the fifth consecutive night that I have had no sleep. I have been averaging three hours of sleep in each twenty-four hour period. Between the coast, and the fishing boats and freighters, there is danger everywhere. The lack of sleep is beginning to tell on me; and I'm certain that I look like something that no one would want to meet in a dark alley.

Radio contact is practically constant now. Everyone seems to be waiting for me: parents, friends, newspapermen. We were picked up by Breguet-Atlantique and talked for a while. Then, at 1645: *land!* Slightly south of Ouessant. If I had not had to tack, I would have turned a somersault.

I have a sounding of 370 feet and, in my ears, sound of the foghorn from the Pierres-Noires.

Wednesday, March 27.

"Tack, tack, tack . . ." It's very easy to make these entries in my log. As easy as our progress is slow. I am trying to use the tide current to enter the Channel, because the wind is still practically nil.

At about 1700, there was a swell from the northwest. It was about time.

By 2100, I was eight miles northwest of Héaux de Breéhat. If the winds hold, I have to go about five miles north-northwest, then head east-southeast to pass between Barnouic and La Horaine. From there, it is a straight course to Saint-Malo. If the wind holds.

Thursday, March 28.

We've done it. The end of the voyage is here, ninety days out of Sydney—days which mingled new records with old problems, little troubles with moments of real anxiety but also with times of pure joy.

Upon setting out last September 8 (in bad weather) for this voyage around the world, my first hope above all was to take *Manureva* round the three great capes and to bring her back safely to her port. I have done that. Then there was the matter of new records, in which, if I say so myself, we did not do badly at all.

This is my last night, and I am spending it on watch: keeping track of the readings on the depth sounder, watching for ships, keeping an eye out for the Dover cliffs, and gnashing my teeth over our four-knot speed. I've also made our final tally: 892 miles, for a total of 15,427. An average of 171.4 nautical miles a day, at an average speed of 7.14 knots.

Finally, at 0640, we are in a calm sea only six miles off Saint-Malo.

These were the closing lines of my log, and they marked the beginning of one of the most beautiful days of my life, one that I will never forget.

The joy of the sailor's life is based on patience and on the ability to wait. It is never complete and whole until he has returned to port. There is all the time in the world, during the long hours that a sailor spends becalmed, to picture the return home. I was no exception; and I imagined my return time after time, with different settings and different dialogue for each occasion. My favorite was the one that had *Manureva* coming into port under full sail, cutting through the spray; and on deck, Alain Colas, freshly washed and shaved, becomingly modest, but with a triumphant heart beating in his manly chest.

The reality of homecoming was quite different. I was exhausted and spent all my time desperately tacking, closehauled, while *Manureva* wandered in the dense fog, being pushed a bit by the swell and pushed another few feet by an occasional feeble gust. And yet, my imagined homecomings all paled into insignificance beside the actuality. I had never seen so many people, a crowd in which I could occasionally distinguish the face of a friend, a wave from a relative, a tight knot of journalists. Certainly, I had expected that I would be the center of attention for a few hours in a small town on the coast of Brittany, if only among those who cared about the sea; but I had never imagined a celebration such as the one that awaited me.

In the excitement of setting foot on dry land again, my first step onto the Dinard jetty almost sent me sprawling on the ground—my foot caught in the hand-rail of the boat that had come to get me from my mooring. Then, walking about the people who had come to meet me, listening to them shouting, touching their outstretched hands, basking in their applause, it occurred to me that, in my old sea clothes and with my sea-man's walk (feet spread to compensate for the pitching and tossing of the deck) I must have looked like nothing so much as a large duck.

On the dock, standing next to one another, were my mother, who was radiant with joy, and Teura, who was dressed in loose clothing which hinted at the joy that she carried in her womb. After sixty-nine days at sea, the voyage was complete. And, at the end of that final week, exhausting because of its sleepless nights and windless days, these few moments of welcome gave to the voyage whatever importance and weight it may have. I had driven myself, and driven myself hard; I had worked, and worked hard; from day to day, I had done my best to fulfill the mission that I had assigned to myself. And now, I suddenly realized how good it was to have done what I set out to do.

Appendix I

Technical information on *Manureva*

Builder:	La Perrière Shipyard, Lorient, France
Designer:	André Allègre
Material:	Baked Aluminum Cegeduz AG4 MC
Length:	69 feet
Beam:	35.7 feet
Draft (with centerboard):	8 feet
Draft (centerboard raised):	4 feet
Length of pontoons:	58.6 feet
Mainmast:	61 feet. Nirvana (Yverdon) spars. Sectional, nirvuanal aluminum Alu Suisse
Mizzenmast:	59 feet. Sectional, nirvuanal aluminum Alu Suisse
Booms:	Sectional, nirvuanal aluminum Alu Suisse. Nirvana spars
Sailmaker:	Victor Tonnerre, Lorient, France

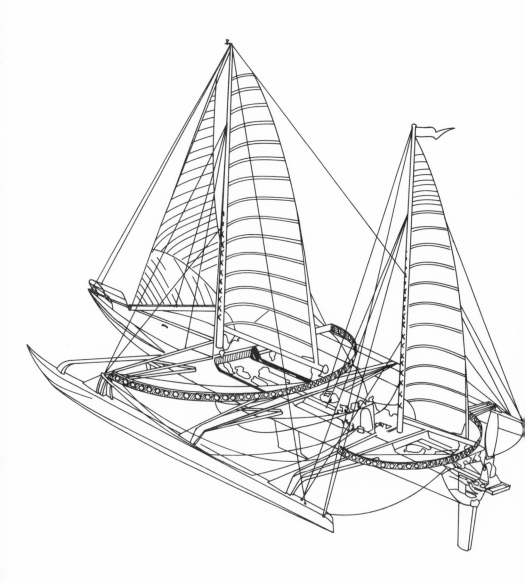

Mainsail with battens:	Dacron, 202 sq. feet, 9.25 oz.
Mizzen with battens:	Dacron, 135 sq. feet, 9.25 oz.
Running jib with battens:	Dacron, 118 sq. feet, 9.25 oz.
Jib #2:	Dacron, 91 sq. feet, 9.25 oz.
Jib #1:	Dacron, 50.5 sq. feet, 9.25 oz.
Storm-jib:	Tergal, 30 sq. feet, 490 g.
Trysail (mainmast):	Tergal, 40 sq. feet, 440 g.
Trysail (mizzenmast):	Tergal, 30 sq. feet, 440 g.
Genoa (light):	Dacron, 236 sq. feet, 4.50 oz.
Genoa (heavy):	Dacron, 168.5 sq. feet, 8.25 oz.
Reaching jib:	Dacron, 360.5 sq. feet, 4.5 oz.
Gennikers (2):	Dacron, 404 sq. feet, 3.5 oz.
Spinnaker (storm):	Nylon, 303 sq. feet, Force 9.
Spinnaker (large):	Nylon, 607 sq. feet, 1.5 oz.
Spinnaker (light):	Nylon, 539 sq. feet, 0.75 oz.
Main staysail:	Nylon, 337 sq. feet, 1.5 oz.
Small staysail:	Tergal, 270 sq. feet, 175 g.
Tallboy:	Tergal, 101 sq. feet, 210 g.
Mizzen staysail:	Tergal, 162 sq. feet, 260 g.
Double-braid lines:	Lancelin, Ernée, France
Rigging, stainless steel	S.A.R.M.A., St-Vallier-sur-Rhône, France
Topsides:	Goiot, Nantes, France
Security equipment:	Plastimo, Lorient, France
Blocks:	Delabie-Gaspard, Belloy, France
Speed-regulator:	Gianoli-Ecca
Standby speed-regulator:	Atoms-MCB
Electric automatic pilot:	Decca-CRM
Radio transmitter:	Clipper 400 watts CRM

Meteorological facsimile:	Tayofax
Sounding apparatus:	Simrad
Radio direction finder:	TDA 259
Compass:	Vion
Sextants:	Vion and Tamaya
Direction and speed anemometer:	GEA 70 MCB
Loch-speedometer:	Brookes and Gatehouse
Mizzen direction and speed anemometer:	Brookes and Gatehouse
Accelerometer:	Modulog Oxy Nautica
Navigation bubble:	Altuglass
Electrical installation:	C.S.E.E.
Generator:	Onan 2 Kva.
Standby generator:	Honda
Hot-air heating:	Schneebeli-Chabaud
Dinghy:	Zodiac Mark II
Outboard motor:	Evinrude 20 hp.
Insulated clothing and sleeping clothing:	Equinoxe
Waterproofing tests:	C.E.A. Pierrelatte
Painting:	International Celomer
Anchorage:	FOB

Appendix 2

Boat Talk

ARM   The tubes or structure that connect the center hull of a trimaran with its pontoons.

ASTRONOMICAL TABLES   Calendar of apparent movements of the sun and other celestial points of reference by means of which the navigator of a vessel in the open sea is able to calculate her position on the ocean.

AUTOMATIC PILOT   An electrical system—usually used on engine-powered boats and ships—which holds a vessel on a predetermined course. A network of relays, solenoids, and contacts controls an electric motor or a central hydraulic system that transmits course corrections to the rudder. This system does not take the wind into account, and it is up to the navigator to adapt and regulate his sail "on demand."

BALLAST   The weight in a boat which gives it stability in the wind. Live ballast is the skipper and his crew, who shift their weight in the boat according to the wind, weather, and direction.

BATTEN   A long, thin strip of wood or plastic inserted into a pocket along the outside edge of a sail to keep it from flapping in the wind.

BEAT   To sail toward the direction from which the wind is blowing, by tacking—that is, zigzagging—from one side to the other.

BLOCK   A grooved wheel rotating in a frame or shell. The frame itself is attached to another object. Various arrangements of blocks can greatly increase the amount of force exerted by a single man handling a line threaded through the blocks.

BOARD BOAT   A small single-hull boat, with a centerboard keel. Since it capsizes with relative ease, the weight of the sailor must be used to maintain its stability.

BOLT ROPE   A line sewn along the edge of a sail. Traditionally, it is of rope.

BOOM   In older days, the boom was made of wood. Today, it is usually a hollow tube of light—and therefore easily manageable—metal. The boom is attached at a right angle to the mast by "jaws" or by a "gooseneck." The boom is always to leeward; that is, on the side of the boat opposite the wind.

BOTTOM   The sides and keel of a boat up to the waterline.

CATAMARAN   A sailboat with two hulls. The catamaran traces its origin to the astonishing migratory voyages of the Malayo–Polynesians across the Pacific.

CENTERBOARD   On *Manureva,* the centerboard is a piece of flat molded aluminum situated in a well. It keeps the boat from slipping sideways (making leeway) in the wind and, while not appreciably reducing the boat's speed, gives it more stability, particularly in rolling seas or rough weather.

CHAINPLATE A structural metal piece of the deck used for securing the metal cables supporting the mast.

CLEAT A two-pronged piece of nautical hardware, permanently bolted to the deck and to spars, around which a line is secured. To cleat a line means to tie it to a cleat.

COCKPIT The well or protected space where the tiller is located and where the crew sits.

COME ABOUT To change a boat's course by turning into the wind, so that the wind then comes on the other side of the sails.

COMPASS An instrument, with a magnetic needle pointing to magnetic north, that is used for determining direction. The compass floats in a sealed bowl mounted on gimbals and therefore remains level at all times.

COMPASS ROSE The compass rose appears on all nautical charts and consists of a set of two circles. The outer circle gives true north; the inner, the related magnetic north for the area illustrated on the chart.

COURSE The direction in which a vessel is sailing. The skipper "sets a course" for a particular destination or point.

CROSS-BAR BEAMS Wooden elements which serve to support the deck.

DECK The platform that covers part of the huli. On the *Manureva,* the foredeck is situated between the stem and the mast.

DIRECTION AND SPEED ANEMOMETER An electronic device located at the top of the mast that measures the direction and force of the wind and records this information on dials in the cockpit for the helmsman's benefit.

DOWNHAUL Line attached to the underside of a boom. It serves to stretch tight the luff, or front edge of a sail, once it has been raised.

DRAFT The draft of a boat is the depth of water needed to float the boat.

EASE, or EASE OFF To loosen; to pay out or slack off. To ease the sheet, for example, is to let out the rope that controls a sail.

FALL OFF To head the boat away from the direction of the wind. The helmsman may also be told to "head away" or "head off."

FOOT The lower edge of a sail next to the boom.

FORE STAYSAIL A small triangular sail sometimes used in place of the jib. It is used frequently in ketch-rigged and schooner-rigged boats.

FURL To roll up and secure a sail to a boom or spanker boom. Jibs are rarely furled, but are stowed in a bag.

GENOA or GENOA JIB A large jib overlapping the mainsail and controlled by sheets outside all the rigging. The genoa is used for racing and to increase speed.

GIANOLI The inventor of the automatic piloting device aboard *Manureva*. I sometimes refer to this device as "the Gianoli" to distinguish it from my alternate automatic pilot, the "Atoms."

GIMBAL A metal contrivance consisting of a number of pivoted rings for suspending an object in such a way that it remains level when its support is tipped. The stove in a boat's galley is usually mounted on gimbals, for example, to keep pots and pans level even if the boat pitches and tosses.

GOOSENECK A metal piece by which the boom is attached to the mast. It allows the boom to swing in all directions.

HALYARD A line or rope used to raise or lower a sail. On larger boats, the halyards are used in combination with winches.

HARNESS System of straps and buckles which form a kind of vest, and which, when attached to fixed brackets by means of a strap or line, is intended as a security measure.

HAUL To haul a line is to pull or take in a line. It is the opposite of easing or paying out a line.

HAULING THE WIND To haul the wind is a maneuver (difficult in a high wind) which turns the boat nearer the wind by progressive stages until it is closehauled.

HEEL The sideways tipping of a boat resulting from wind in sails. The boat heels particularly when you are closehauled and beating. If the wind is too strong, or if you have too much sail, heeling could result in capsizing. Archimedes, however, takes care of multihulled boats, and his colleague, Newton, watches over single-hulls and other keeled boats that are duly ballasted.

INNER PLANKING The interior siding of a boat which runs perpendicular to the keel.

JIB The queen of sails in front of the mast. The jib is triangular in shape. In size, it runs from the little storm jib to the large running jib.

JIBE   To jibe is to turn the boat's stern in such a way that the wind comes on the other side of the sails by crossing behind rather than in front of the boat. The purpose of this maneuver is to change course, or to hold to one's course when the wind has shifted. Jibing necessitates getting the sails from one side of the boat to the other. This maneuver requires vigilance and coordination. A jibe can be intentional or unintentional, the latter occurring when the wind crosses the stern and begins blowing on the same side the sail is on without the skipper's noticing it. An unplanned jibe can be disastrous.

LATITUDE   Latitude, along with longitude, provides geographic coordinates of everything on earth. It is the angular distance, north or south from the Equator, of an object, measured by parallels running from 0° to 90° from the Equator to the two poles. For that reason, latitudes are always given as north or south.

LAY TO   A sailor "lays to" or "lies to" when he turns his boat into the wind and keeps it there—in bad weather, for example—to neutralize the effect of the wind on the sails. In such instances, one may use a "sea anchor," which resembles a kind of large funnel the mouth of which is held open by an arch-shaped piece of steel or by a wooden cross-bar. The floating anchor, when secured to the bow, serves to keep the boat turned into the wind; and, when secured to the stern, it brakes the movement of the boat in the current.

LEECH   Outside edge of a sail farthest from the mast, into which the leech line is sewed. The latter is used to regulate flapping in the leech.

LIFT   The line supporting a spar such as the mainsail boom or the spinnaker pole.

LINE   A generic nautical term for almost all ropes used on a boat. Thus, one "secures" the anchor, the boom, or the lifeboat with "lines."

LOCH   An electronic odometer which is tied in to a small propellor or electrodes under the hull and which measures the distance traveled.

LONGITUDE   The arc of the Equator intercepted between, or the angle between, the meridian of a given place and a prime meridian, as that of Greenwich, England. Any given spot on earth is at the center of a gigantic cross; and that point is located by describing its position as being so many degrees and minutes of longitude east or west, and so many degrees and minutes of latitude north or south.

LUFF   A sail luffs when it shakes as the wind is spilled out of it, with the result that the boat is slowed so as to facilitate a maneuver. You can luff simply by turning the boat into the wind with the tiller, or by letting out the sail.

MIZZENMAST   The after mast in a ketch or yawl.

NAUTICAL MILE   A nautical mile is the equivalent to a minute of longitude at the Equator and is longer than a land mile, being 6,080.20 feet (in the U.S. The British "Admiralty Mile" is 6,080.00 feet). The term "knot" goes back to the days when speed was measured by trailing a line in the wake with regularly spaced knots in it.

PLANING   Like surfing: going through the water faster than the waves.

RADIO DIRECTION FINDER   An instrument which makes it possible to establish one's location with respect to a broadcast beam.

RADIO-TELEPHONE B.L.U. A short-wave device for long distance communication at high frequency (4 to 23 megacycles).

REEF To reduce the area of a sail.

RIGGING The wires and ropes that hold up the masts and control the sails.

ROLLER-REEFING My gennikers, which were large genoa jibs, were reefed by means of a winch that rolled up the genniker from the bottom and reduced its surface. Mainsails can also be roller-reefed, in which case the boom is rotated with a cranking device so that the sail wraps around it.

ROPE Cord made of twisted fibers or metal strands which, when used on a sailboat, is known generically as "line."

RUN FREE To run free is to sail before the wind; i.e., with the wind behind, or aft.

RUNNING BACKSTAY Adjustable line supporting the mast used especially when running before the wind.

SAIL TRACK A metal strip or track along the mast or boom. The sail is fitted into the sail track by slides, or lugs, sewn onto the edge of the sail.

SET OF THE SAILS As the wind shifts aft of the boat, the set of the sails goes successively from closehauled, close reach, beam reach, and broad reaching, to running before the wind. In the latter case, beware of accidental jibing.

SHACKLE A device used for fastening, for example, the end of a halyard to a sail. The standard shackle is U-shaped, with a removable pin across the open end.

SHEET   A rope or line attached to the aft corner (clew) of a sail by which the sail is let out or pulled in according to the direction and force of the wind.

SHROUD   A wire support providing lateral support to the mast. They run from the upper part of the mast to the sides of the boat.

SLIDES   Small metal or plastic lugs used to attach the front edge and bottom of a sail (mainsail, jib, or foresail) to its mast or stay. The slides are sewn or otherwise attached to the edge of the sail and inserted into the sail track running along the mast or boom.

SOUND   To measure the depth of water. A modern sounding apparatus, or sonar, measures depth in relation to the time that is required to receive an echo from a signal transmitted. The reading is given in feet, meters, or fathoms.

SPEED REGULATOR   This is a wholly mechanical piloting system which is often, and erroneously, described as "automatic." What it actually does is regulate the speed of a sailboat with respect to the direction of the wind by making use of the wind's action on a small vane or rib made of wood or plastic, which is called the aerial, or aerial element. Once a boat is on the proper course, the aerial is mounted on its bracket aft, in such a way that its edge faces the wind. As long as the boat remains on course, nothing happens. If the boat begins to wander, the change of the wind on the aerial transmits a message directly to the "Fletner shutters" on the rudder (Gianoli system) or to the submerged paddle (Atoms system). The tiller-ropes will then adjust the tiller accordingly. The effectiveness of either system obviously depends on whether or not the force of the water striking either the shutters or the paddle corresponds to the force needed to make the proper correction.

SPINNAKER The spinnaker is a large, light spherical sail, often in bright colors, which is usually used when going before the wind. It effectively almost doubles the sail area.

SPINNAKER POLE LIFT Line from mast to the middle of a spinnaker pole which serves to hold the pole in place.

STAY An element of the standing rigging, usually of stainless steel, used to support the mast. It runs lengthwise to the bow or stern.

SWIFTER An aft shroud secured to the head of the mast. It is often used as a radio antenna.

TACK To tack is to sail a zigzag course into the wind; that is, to sail close to the wind in a zigzag direction. It also means going from a port tack (with the wind coming from the left side) to a starboard tack (with the wind from the right side).

TILLER The steering device of the boat. A wooden or metal arm by which the rudder is controlled.

TIMBERS A term used in naval construction to designate the ribs of a ship. In fact, if the frame of a ship corresponded to the human skeleton, the timbers would be the ribs.

VEER To change course by turning away from the wind.

WATCH The interval of time during which a sailor is ''on duty'' to man the tiller and do shipboard chores.

WIND SCALE A scale for wind measurement invented in 1805 by Admiral Sir Francis Beaufort. The Beaufort scale measures wind by ''force,'' running from ''force 0'' (calm) to force 12 (hurricane). At force 8, the wind is really beginning to blow; and anything above force 10 means very serious problems indeed.

YAWL   A type of rigging characterized by two masts, with the smaller mast set back of the rudder stock.

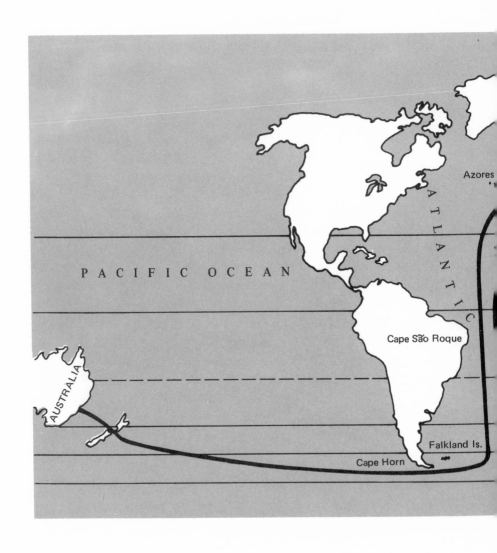

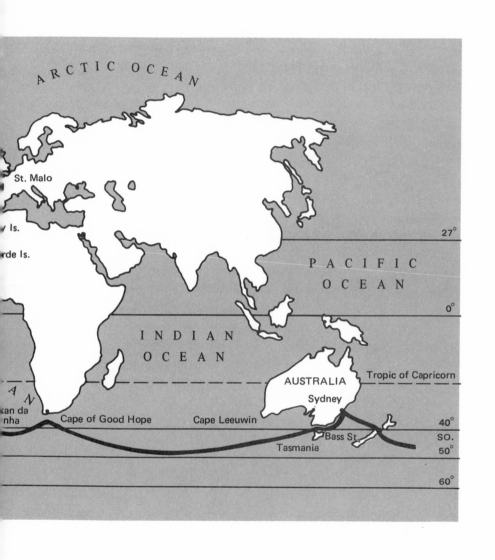

ARCTIC OCEAN

St. Malo

Is.

rde Is.

PACIFIC
OCEAN

27°

0°

INDIAN
OCEAN

Tropic of Capricorn

AUSTRALIA
Sydney

A
N

kan da
nha   Cape of Good Hope   Cape Leeuwin

40°

Bass St.   SO.

Tasmania   50°

60°

The most lavish and complete book on pleasure boating ever published!

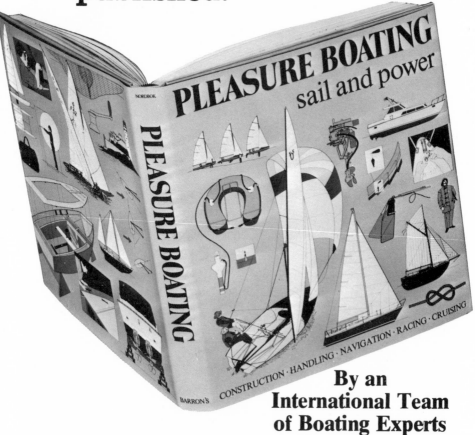

By an International Team of Boating Experts

The beginner, the intermediate, and the experienced boating enthusiast will appreciate the scope and detail of this visually exciting book. Packed with information and advice, it will become every boatman's all-purpose, all-year-round reference.

Covers the basics of rigging, navigation, and equipment through inshore, offshore, and transatlantic racing. Over 1400 drawings in color and line; many cross-sectional views. Everything the sailor or powerboater needs on land or off. Size: 10¾ x 11⅞ in. 280 pp.

$29.95 cloth, at your bookstore, or send check to **Barron's**, Woodbury, N.Y. 11797. Add 85¢ transportation charges. **N.Y.** and **N.J.** residents, add sales tax. Return book within **15 days** if not satisfied for full refund.

The goal of this handbook is to explain that waxing is not so complicated, tedious, and difficult to manage successfully, and that any skier can learn to wax well.
$1.95 paper

Style is the subject of this book. It begins where most ski books leave off — with parallel skiing — and teaches the techniques that make a competent skier into a very good skier. $5.95 paper

Chester Barnes' object in writing this book was to describe methods of play as he has come to understand them as a champion, and to encourage newcomers to try their hand at this exhilarating game. $4.95 hardcover

Expert Celia Brackenridge shares her knowledge and skills in this fast-paced game. Intended to teach an effective way of playing lacrosse, this book looks at all aspects of the sport in relation to the game and game situations, rather than isolation.
$4.95 hardcover

Olympic Gold Medalist Jean-Claude Killy and French ski coach Honoré Bonnet cover everything from beginning instruction to après-ski camaraderie. Sequence photos show how to do the snow plow, christies, turns, sidesliding, wedelns, avalement, and more.
$12.95 hardcover

A champion and an experienced coach with knowledge of all aspects of field hockey, Rachael Heyhoe Flint gives sound advice on the techniques and method of play, which is enhanced by excellent action photos.
$4.95 hardcover